the Casual CONSERVATIONIST

the little green book of proven ideas
and practical ideals for leading a better life

ERIC MONGO ROBBINS

Author – Eric Mongo Robbins
Publicette – Adrienne Biggs (www.BiggsPublicity.com)
Cover and Layout – Toolbox Creative (www.toolboxcreative.com)
The Artsy Folks – Kevin Coffey (www.cartoonlandanimation.com),
Rachael Cudmore, Brandy Murad, and
Jessica Milne (www.jessicamilne.com)
HowToConserve.com Web Design – Calvin Chan (www.CalvinChan.net)
Video Dude – Rudy Gelenter (www.RudyPictures.com) and maybe you too?
Co-pilot – Dog

Published by Windswept Words, LLC,
an independent publisher of wind-tested literature
Printed in the United States of America

ISBN 10-dig: 0-9797274-0-5
ISBN 13-dig: 978-0-9797274-0-5

Look out below!!

Table of Contents

Legal Stuff 2

THE BEGINNING: WHO IS MONGO AND WHAT ON EARTH POSSESSED HIM TO WRITE THIS BOOK? 7

STAGE 1

How to Read This Book 13

STAGE 2

The Argument 19

STAGE 3

The Way of the Casual Conservationist. 25

The Steps of Stuff (very important!) 30

STAGE 4

The Goods (At Home). 37

CHAPTER 1: WHAT A WASTE! 37

Bag-Packs 38

Dogs Rule 39

Recycle Big and Loud 39

Paper versus Plastic 42

The Considerate Kitchen 44

Feeling Pickled 45

Garden Goodies 47

CHAPTER 2: WATER, WATER EVERYWHERE 49
More Garden Goodies 50
Shower Time! 51
Back to the Basins 52
Eau de Toilet 53
Dish It Up 55
Laundering the Green 57
Pit Check 57
Gray Waters 58

CHAPTER 3: PAYING THE BILLS & OTHER PAPER CHASES 61
Let Your Fingers Do the Walking 61
The Paperless Office 63
Nose Mud 64

CHAPTER 4: ENERGY DRUNK 65
Air Raid 65
Power Down 67
Trip the Lights 70

CHAPTER 5: THE GIFT ECONOMY 71
Wrap It Up 76
Gift Allies 76

CHAPTER 6: OTHER STUFF 77
Moving On Up 77
Feel of the Cloth 78
Naïve Bottling 78

CHAPTER 7: THE HOME GAME 81
Do-It-Yourself Stickers 83-85

STAGE 5
The Goods (On the Road) 89

CHAPTER 8: EATING OUT 89
Double-Cupped Coffee 90
The Law of Conservation Probability 90
Dining at Work 91

CHAPTER 9: OTHER STUFF 93
Smoke 'Em If You Got 'Em 93
Trash Walks 94
Trash Hash 95
If I say it's safe to surf this beach... 95
Commute Your Commute 96
Public Transportation 97

CHAPTER 10: NOISE POLLUTION 101
Honk! 101
Leaf Blowers 102
Cell Phones 102

CHAPTER 11: ROAD TRIPPING GAMES FOR THE KIDS 103
Are We There Yet? 103
License Plate Game Re-Dub 105
Name That Tree 105
Capture the Schwag 106
Plus many more! 105-107

STAGE 6
Talking and Walking Conservation 109

CHAPTER 12: GET YOUR FEET IN THE DIRT (INSERT NATURE HERE) 109

CHAPTER 13: THE CRAFT OF THE CASUAL CONSERVATIONIST 113

CHAPTER 14: THE CASUAL CONSERVATION CORPS 119

CHAPTER 15: THE CODE OF THE CASUAL CONSERVATION CORPS 123

THE END 127

More Lessons 127-131

Fun With Cats 127

When the Great Outdoors Come Indoors 128

Know Your Geography 128

Conserve Our Traditions 129

Girlfriend Games 130

Minimal Effort Night (MEN) 131

Mind Conservation 131

Conserve Your Teeth 133

THE END! 135

More Rants 135-142

Self Reliance 135

Conservation versus Capitalism 136

No Presents? 142

THE END? 145

What is *energy* and what does it have to do with *greenhouses*? 145

Green Attitudes Deserve Gratitudes 150

BLANK JOURNAL PAGE 154

ABOUT THE AUTHOR 155

END NOTES 157

THE BEGINNING

Who is Mongo and what on earth possessed him to write this book?

Hello. My name is Mongo. And what you are about to read contains revolutionary ideas that, once upon a time in America, were commonplace. Four Decembers ago, I was strapped for cash, short on time and dreading the idea of buying quick, convenient holiday gifts for people that would probably end up in the garbage can soon after. So I decided to break the rules for the first time in my life. I wrote a short book entitled, *Get Mean and Go Green.* In it, I shared the fun and easy ways that I conserve natural resources like water, trees and oil around the house and on the road. I printed 20 copies – no plastic wrap, gift paper or holiday cards needed – and gave them out to my friends and my family. Everyone seemed to love the gift and the whole thing only cost me 150 bucks!

Three years passed by and I found myself at another crossroads – commuting two hours a day to work and hearing daily news stories about how my lifestyle was causing the glaciers to melt, the seas to rise and the earth to warm. Yep, everybody was talking about *global warming* and *climate change.* And it occurred to me that, if what I was hearing was true, nothing I did from this moment on would matter unless something changed...unless I changed. I could work hard my entire life – buy a house, raise some children, help them raise their kids – and it could all wash away 5, 10, 20 years from now...literally.

Not being one to back down from an important fight, I dove headfirst into the rising sea of information spewing out on the television, radio and the Internet. It was like drinking from a fire hose. I attended Earth Day Conferences, recycling classes and fact-finding symposiums put on by the Mathematical Sciences Research Institute. I learned about alternative energy, new technologies and best practices of the environmentally enlightened. Along the way, I discovered a lot of solutions – some good, some bad and some that just wouldn't work for busy Americans who had mortgages to pay and kids to feed.

Then I met this fella named Dog who was the tipping point for me. He told me I was lucky because most people don't have the time or energy to learn about these things. Furthermore, Dog told me that I had an *obligation* to teach what I had learned. Nobody had ever said this to me before! So I promised Dog that I would teach what I knew. But I couldn't just thump people over the head with global warming statistics. I needed to empower people with solutions tailored to their increasingly busy lives.

But it's hard. It is hard to know which solutions are actually good for the earth and which solutions just *look good.* There are a lot of feel-good, well-meaning solutions out there that have crawled their way into the consumer mind, fueled by advertising dollars and our collective guilt for the way we have treated our mountains and oceans.

There are vitamin supplements that somehow save the rainforests. There is the gas station boycott that pops into your email inbox every now and then, which is the butt of jokes among economists and all thinking people.

But I didn't come here today to point a finger at the bad ideas. I came here to point my finger at the good ideas and to teach you how to spot the goodies so that you can identify them when I'm long gone. To that end, I have created an identification system called the *Steps of Stuff* to help you make smart, green-friendly consumption decisions for you and your family. You don't need to be an expert in green house emissions or alternative fuels to understand how to spot a goody.

In this book, I also aim to make you think differently about conservation. I aim to expand your mind to the possibility that life can be better for you and your family – now and in the future – using *conservation* as your life compass. I aim to define conservation more broadly than it has been defined in the past. You see, conservation is not just about recycling stuff – recycling is good but there are better ways. And I aim to have a little fun. I hope my aim is true with you. Whether you decide to join me in this journey by reading this book or having a conversation with me as I tour over 500 American cities this summer and fall, I hope you will learn a little and teach your friends and family to aim well too.

Lastly, I'm not an expert in the environmental sciences, nor am I a credentialed teacher. But I am a thinking man and a passionate man – passionate about leaving this earth a little bit better that I found her. That is why I decided to tour America using my own money and resources...to share what I have learned and to discover what I have yet to learn. Feel free to join me in this journey on my website www.HowToConserve.com or just come out to talk with me when I'm passing near your town. But don't delay! My time on this earth is short and I have promises to keep. And I can't do this without you.

Casually Yours,

Mongo

Eric Mongo Robbins
Your Son, Grandson, Nephew, Uncle, Cousin,
Colleague, Neighbor and Friend

"Be the change you want to see in the world... whatever you do will be insignificant, but it is very important that you do it."

– Bapu, a leader know better by another name

STAGE 1
How to Read This Book...

Upside down¿

The Casual Conservationist has found you. You can put this book down and run away but there is no one to save you from...*the future.* Muhahahahahahaha! *There is no wrought-iron safe keeping, nor cuddled Pinkerton to insure amens.* But don't be afraid – this is not a technical book, although there are some researched facts 'n figures that will strike fear deep into the hearts of your parting party guests. It is a human book, a book of the living, a book that can transform your life...if you will it. It has changed my life in writing it. It is a con**ver**sation about con**ser**vation for people who would really like to change the world without spending too much change, without spending too much time, because we all lead busy lives. Breathe. Don't waste this opportunity to change your world a little and I promise you'll have more time and more fun while saving what's left of Heaven on earth.

The Casual Conservationist was never meant to be read...but to be read with relish, poured over powerfully, glanced at gingerly, written in wantonly, and cut up carefully. You will need a pen, a pair of scissors, sticky tape...and curiosity. You will not need any fear or trepidation. Bring a dictionary, unless of course you fear words like 'trepidation'. Some words you will not find in the dictionary. Don't worry, I made them up.

You may choose to buy *The Casual Conservationist*, the e-book, the radio interviews, the Anniversary Edition Spoon Warmers, or to just sit there browsing for free. Hey, this is not a library! Or maybe it is? However these words find you, for however long they find you, know that I love you, or at least like you a lot...even if you don't buy my Spoon Warmers. I just ask one thing of you: write down one lesson in this book, write now. Then go home and do it. I promise it will cost you about a dime on your time and you will have stopped running away.

The Casual Conservationist is meant to be imitated, exercised, reshaped and recreated...at home, on your walkabouts and while on long road-trips with the kids. **This is a great book for road trips!** For the kids or the kid in you, I have added a section dedicated to road-tripping games. What does that have to do with 'conservation', you may ask? Just rearrange the letters and you get the word *conversation.* Road games are about the *conservation of conversation.* Aha! Next road trip, instead of asking how much of your time is left, ask how much of your mind is left. For a free, easy-to-print copy of these games, go to www.HowToConserve.com or bring this book with you on the road. ROAD TRIP!

The Casual Conservationist is one part fact, mixed in with a bunch of creative conservation ideas from people all over America. That means some of the book is real and some is pretty surreal. You can usually tell when I'm joking around. However, use your best judgment when encountering information or a word you believe to be susspecked.

The Casual Conservationist is one part 'how-to' manual for the lazy-busy people of the world who have little time or money to save the planet. I include myself in your ranks, thank you very much.

The Casual Conservationist is one part children's game to get them to brush their teeth and take out the recycle bin, all the while saving you money! Think of this book as a guide to entertaining your kids while secretly putting them to work and teaching them something. Think Tom Sawyer and the picket fence.

The Casual Conservationist is one part journal for you to write your own conservational thoughts and ideas as they appear in your head. Don't hesitate. Thoughts are like dreams in this way. If you don't write them down immediately after waking, they drift away. You are the creator, the lover, the dreamer and me.

And lastly, *The Casual Conservationist* is one part the semi-coherent rants of a wild-eyed spendthrift and *straphanger* named Mongo. Check out the end of the book to see who you are dealing with. Be careful, he looks hungry!

Lazy-busy people of the world: READ THIS BOOK!

Read it. Don't question my author-ih-tee. Well, always question authority...except mine, which consists of nothing more than my sweet ear-eye-heart sense-abilities.

You CAN read, can't you? If not, go to www.HowToConserve.com and listen to the audio-book. What, can't hear? Then I say loudly, READ THIS BOOK!

Give the gift of good word. *The Casual Conservationist* makes a great Christmas stocking stuffer, Barmitzfa booty, first fruit of Kwanzaa, Blessed Rainy Day bounty, Jul jewel, Naw-Ruz remembrance, Holi handout, or Boxer's Day knockout.

Steady now! Ready now?

"I am the eagle, I live in high country
In rocky cathedrals that reach to the sky.
I am the hawk and there's blood on my feathers
But time is still turning they soon will be dry.
And all of those who see me, all who believe in me
Share in the freedom I feel when I fly!
Come dance with the west wind and touch on the
mountain tops,
Sail o'er the canyons and up to the stars.
And reach for the heavens and hope for the future
And all that we can be and not what we are."

– John Denver, The Eagle and the Hawk

STAGE 2
The Argument

Global Warming is not real. Al Gore doesn't know what he's talking about. And hasn't he gained a few inconvenient pounds?

The majority of scientists[1]: "The earth, water and air are getting warmer. And Al Gore looks just fine."

So it's getting warmer. Big deal! Global warming is a natural trend — nature's thermostat at work. Certainly, she has a master plan in mind!?

The majority of scientists: "It's true that throughout history, the earth's temperatures have fluctuated between hot and cold times. These are natural cycles. It's also true that it's getting warmer and odds are real good that man is contributing to this effect through his burning of fossil fuels and other stuff. You see, it works like this: we survive the cold temperatures of space because light from the sun bounces off the ground you walk on and back into space, warming the ground, air and the top of your head. If it didn't bounce back into space and stuck around instead, we would all be fried bananas. Similarly, if too much bounced off our upper atmosphere, we would all be banana-sickles. Our waste – the carbon dioxide, methane and nitrous oxide emissions from driving cars and other human activities – is creating a layer in the sky that allows sunlight in, but won't let it all out, like the windows of a green house, so it sticks around and heats up the air and ground again and again."

I haven't noticed any changes around my house. The water still works, the food keeps appearing in the refrigerator. I still play with the kids in the sunshine and we don't all fry like eggs over-easy. What gives?

The majority of scientists: "Historically speaking, this trend of atmospheric heating is accelerating – that means it's heating faster every year. Maybe faster than the earth's natural thermostat can handle. We don't know that, yet. But it's happening slowly in your mind because you have a short attention span. It's not your fault, human. You don't live long enough to really see the long-term effects and your children and their children are born with a new frame of reference each generation. That means they see only the changes that occur during their lifetimes. Couple that with the fact you actually have a short attention span borne of a busy life and watching too much television and you can imagine how easily you missed this warming trend."

Ok, fine. So what do I care if it gets a little warmer? I mean, it's darn cold in winter where I live and I could really save some coin if it were warmer. I don't live on the coast, so why should I care if Britney Malibu has to swim from her mansion to the mail box because sea levels have risen? I don't go on safari so why should I care if a few mean old tigers have gone extinct? I don't ski so what do I care if a bunch of over-privileged ski-bunnies land on rocks instead of snow?

The majority of scientists: "You don't like to ski?"

Look, I get my drinking water from a local reservoir so what do I care if the rise in sea levels spices up freshwater deltas, destroying tap water for millions of people? I get my food from a never-ending source called the supermarket so what do I care if extreme drought and extreme rainfall prevents farmers all over the world from making enough food? I don't breathe that much air so what do I care if 90% of the world's source of oxygen, the phytoplankton, are in danger of dying off because of warmer ocean waters? What do I care if the remaining air is sooty-smoggy-smelly?

The majority of scientists: "You really don't like to ski? Man that's sick. Is it the tight pants? That was a '70s thing that stuck around. You know, you can wear baggy pants if you want."

Look, if what you say is true, short of jumping off a cliff, I can't make a difference. I have a job and a family to support. I have bills to pay, you know — the bills that kill. This leaves me little time and no money to save the planet. Don't get me wrong, I love the planet. I love life. But you are asking a lot.

The majority of scientists: "We're not asking for anything. It may be too late to stop. Nobody is really sure how the earth might react to this trend. This may all just be an exercise in futility."

Whoa, hold on a minute! I may have a few dollars and a couple of minutes to spare for the earth. Tell me what to do?!

The majority of scientists: "The earth doesn't want your money, nor does she want your time – she'll take that when she's good and ready. Nope, nothing you can do."

Well, I heard the government was researching a theory that giant, reflective plates in space could deflect some of the light.

What if I got all my neighbors together and we all shaved our heads, varnished up our chrome domes and hung out in the sun all day?

The majority of scientists: "Besides being the weirdest idea ever, it won't work. You would have to physically be in orbit, above the atmosphere and without a spacesuit, you might find that a tad uncomfortable. Plus, you would explode. Nope, you're pretty much screwed."

What about the government? Can't we rely on them and modern technology to save us all?

The majority of scientists: "Actually, some of the technology available to us looks pretty promising. It is totally worth spending the time and money to research these promises in the hope of finding a way to fix things. But a promise is not a solution and we have no idea what the side effects will be. They could be worse than the solution itself! We cannot rely on some unknown thing to save us. We should hope for the best but prepare for the worst."

What if everyone reduced the size of their ecological footprint by consuming fewer natural resources like oil, paper and air?

The majority of scientists: "You need to breathe tomorrow as much air as you are breathing today. What are you gonna do, quit your job? Stop driving to work? Stop feeding your family? Stop paying your mortgage?

Nah, the wife would kill me and the children would snack on my remains, like those spiders you see on Animal Planet. So let me get this straight. If I continue to live the way I live, life as I know it might end?!

The majority of scientists: "Yup."

And if I stop going to work, life as I know it might end?!

The majority of scientists: "Yup. We call dibs on the wings."

Well then, I seem to be in pickle. I love my wife and kids but without air to breathe and water to drink, my love won't matter all that much, now will it?

The majority of scientists: "Ahh, now you get it. You have adopted a lifestyle that is likely contributing to warming temperatures and other serious worldly ills. And lifestyles are particularly difficult types of habits to change. They keep you fed and clothed and put a roof over your head. And if it ain't broke, why fix it?"

My dad used that expression all the time! And I've worked really hard to afford this house, buy these cars and clothes for my family.

The majority of scientists: "And we can sympathize with you. We worked hard too but the lifestyle you now *lead* is not the only lifestyle that can provide you with the things you *need.* You have a choice."

What, you think I should go live in a teepee, living off the land? What kind of choice is that?

The majority of scientists: "No, that time has come and gone. There are not enough free roaming animals to hunt and you would get arrested for poaching on private land or in a public park. Plus you have no idea how to farm or find wild, winter potatoes."

I could find a potato.

The majority of scientists: "Sure you could, Spud. However, the point is that, unless you are willing and able to radically change this lifestyle you have built, you must work to change within the bounds of the present system for feeding your family and providing a roof over your head...and that's cool."

That's cool? But I thought my lifestyle was contributing to the fall of my lifestyle?

The majority of scientists: "Mongo, you want to take this one?"

Mongo: "Thanks. Some folks have chosen to radically change their lifestyles and I enthusiastically applaud their efforts to reduce the size of their footprints on this earth. But the majority of people cannot make this leap because the gorge is too wide—they have obligations, responsibilities and promises they need to keep. *The Casual Conservationist* is here to help them keep those promises by bridging the divide one manageable step at a time so they too can reduce their footprints and participate more in this adventure called *conservation.*"

Will you teach me what I need to know?

Mongo: "Let us begin with *The Way.*"

STAGE 3

The Way of the Casual Conservationist

I am the Casual Conservationist and this is my Way. First off, I would like to talk about how stuff gets into your hands. Stuff begins as baby raw materials – iron ore, oil, and imagination. There is a lot of energy used to mine these materials. Tractors burn oil digging and workers sweat hauling. Then there is more energy used to combine these materials into something useful like cars, air conditioners or spoon warmers. Industrial plants burn coal, tires or natural gas to fuel their creations and use water to cool those amazing machines. Then there is even more energy used to ship the resulting spoon warmers to a local retail store to which you have spent still more energy traveling so you can spend the money you earned by sweating your own energy working in the mines.

All this activity takes a lot of energy which leaves a "footprint" on our environment. This footprint is the sum of the effects of these activities, including all the waste products released into our air, attics, oceans, landfills and costly storage units. This is the way the world works, for better or worse. It keeps many people fed and puts a roof over their heads. Without it, you might all be living on the streets...if there were even streets without all this activity.

So when we talk about conservation, I ask that you be mindful of the fact that those spoon warmers you just bought are *the result of* a huge amount of energy being spent on behalf of a whole lot of people and *result in* a huge amount of energy needed for disposal. Even those lumpy street corner couches eventually find their way to the dump in the back of someone's truck.

There is an attitude in this country that buying less is the answer to the problems of climate change and the destruction of our way of life. And what is 'our way of life'? To me, it is children having the opportunity to be children, until it is time for them to be adults. It is parents working hard to ensure their kids get a better education, a better start in life than they had. It is enjoying the fruits of your labor how you want, when you want, without treading on the enjoyment of others. It is the freedom to practice your religious beliefs without intolerance from the government. It is a walk to your local market without fear of harassment or criminal attack. It is life, liberty and the pursuit of happiness. This was the whole point of starting a country and creating The Constitution to protect these rights. Why else have we worked so hard?

But the 'life' part of our American Way is not so certain anymore. How can our children play when there is no clean, outdoor place to play? How can you enjoy the fruits of your labor if there is no clean water to drink and no food on the table? How can you practice your religious beliefs when you can't even breathe? Some of these scenarios are in the process of happening today, right here in America. Some of these scenarios have already happened in other countries around the world like Linfen City, China and La Oroya, Peru. All these scenarios are coming to your city in the not too distant future unless things change.

So I am not asking that you stop buying the stuff you want and need in life. But I am asking that you consider what's *really* important, what 'quality of life' really means to *you.* Please think about the consequences of your consumption decisions not only on your neighborhood, town, state and country, but on the world as a whole because our actions affect farmers in China *as well as* farmers in America.

This may seem like a complex and difficult task but if you take it one step at a time, one purchase at a time, you will find it gets easier with time. And time is what we are buying here. We are buying more time for our children and their children.

Okay, enough doom and gloom. Let's talk solutions. What exactly am I talking about when I use the word *conservation?*

Conservation, noun, (kon-ser-vey-shuh n): "The careful utilization of a natural resource in order to prevent depletion."[2] This is different than preservation.

Preservation, noun, (prez-er-vey-shuh n): "Keeping something in perfect or unaltered condition; maintaining unchanged."[3]

This is but one definition of preservation. There are several others that closely mimic the definition of conservation. And in many ways, these words are the same. But the BIG difference is that conservation is about 'careful utilization', while preservation is about 'keeping something unaltered'. Hikers and hunters understand this difference.

Hikers go exploring in the hundreds of national parks that Big Papa Bear American President Teddy Roosevelt reserved for our use. We walk into nature, sometimes for hours, just to find that perfect view or some lonesome waterfall. We sleep out under the stars and tell stories around the campfire, except during fire season when we tell stories around the flashlight. We fish and watch birds. We try not to get poison oak on our bums. If we encounter bears or boy scouts, we back away cautiously. There's no more dangerous wild animal than a badge-seeking boy scout all hopped up on graham crackers and chocolate bars. And when we head back for our car, we leave no trace – no outward sign of our having been there. This is an example of *the careful utilization of a natural resource.*

Hunters also go exploring in some of our national forests and wetlands – with the intent of bringing home more food than they brought in. When I hunt pheasant, not only do I eat the bird, but I give the tail feathers of the male pheasant to my fishing buddies who turn them into artificial flies. The hunting system in most American states limits the number of animals a hunter can bag and eat. This ensures that the herds of wild animals don't go extinct and are around for future generations of hunters and hikers alike. And the state hunting fees are used to care for and protect the wilds of America. This too is an example *the careful utilization of a natural resource.* Even if you are against the idea of hunting animals, it's hard to miss the harmony inherent between the American-style of hunting and conservation.

So I believe the word preservation is best suited for museums and canned fruits. It is about keeping the land unaltered, untouched and unattainable. And when no one can use the land, what's the point of fighting for it? On the other hand, 'conservation' suggests a need to *participate* in the intelligent and careful use of the land. And that is what we are here for: to *participate* in changing our world by changing our daily lives.

The Way of The Casual Conservationist is a way to *participate* in reducing the energy needed to create and destroy the stuff we buy. There is no room for tourists, voyeurs or other vacant stares in The Way – you must be a participant. But oftentimes it is hard to tell how much energy and waste is being used to create some *thing.* Manufacturers do not label their products with how much water, oil or coal was consumed in the creation of those products. You often don't know what kind of toxic chemicals were used. Even when this information is made public, it is hard to remember it when you actually do go shopping. I know it is for me.

So the last few years, I have begun to look at the things I buy a little differently. I *try* to make purchase decisions based on how much energy and waste products go into their creation. But when I'm not sure, I want to know where some thing is going after I am done using it. What does the afterlife of this *thing* look like? And I rely on a road map that gives me the answer I need. I call this map, *The Steps of Stuff.*

The Steps of Stuff

Whenever you get a hold of some *thing*, ask yourself *these* questions, in *this* order:

Can I re-use it? Using stuff two times or more is *the most efficient method* of conservation. There is no extra energy being used in either the recycling or disposal of this *thing*. If I buy new luggage, will I be able to use it over and over again or will it fall apart in three months? What about the packaging and the bags that it comes in? The paper and plastic bags you get from the grocery store also fall into this category. I see my neighbors using these bags a second time at the grocery store. They securely tie them to garbage cans in areas where people walk their dogs and need doggy bags to scoop the poop. They make good shoe rubbers for when it rains. Parachute? No. But what about stuff you bought a while ago that is no longer perfect like a torn t-shirt? Reuse it as a kitchen rag. This reuse 'philosophy' is the foundation of what it means to be a Casual Conservationist. Plus you save time and money. You don't have to drive to the store once again and spend your money – your *home* is the market!

*Can I **re-gift** it to a friend?* Gifting your *good* stuff to a friend or family member is the ultimate expression of love and fellowship. This can be tough since re-gifting has such a negative image in our society. However, your true friends will appreciate the fact you test-drove their gift to see if it works. When I was younger, I picked up the derogatory expression 'Indian Giver', that somehow the First Nationers and North American Indians had the *bad* habit of re-gifting. It is true...that the elders would invite friends and family to powwows where the elders would re-gift blankets and canoes to their younger party guests. This was a way for the elders to share in their abundance, promote the longevity of the tribe and party between the rocks and stars. Tell you what, a guy gives me a canoe and he better have tested it out on the water more than once or I'm never going to another one of his parties again!

*Can I **re-gift** it to a stranger?* Fell out of love with your t-shirt? Donate it to a thrift store so your t-shirt finds its way onto the arms of someone who may actually 'ski naked', like me. There are tons of folks who shop thrift stores as their primary means of acquiring the stuff they need in life – pots and pans, furniture, clothing and electronics.

You may not like shopping there, which is okay, but your re-gift will help those who do – like me.

*Can I **re-fuse** it?* Some stuff you don't need, like those plastic bags at the corner store used to carry the paper box containing the plastic bottle of cough syrup. Are your hands really that full? Bring a backpack or an oversized purse. Use your pockets. Don't worry, the plastic bag won't be lonely or go to waste – someone else will make sure of that.

Can I re-cycle it? The reason recycling falls in the middle of *The Steps of Stuff* is that there is more energy spent delivering cans, bottles and paper to a recycle center and then more energy washing and melting them down so they can be used once more as the raw materials for other stuff. However, we are all better off when you recycle than when you trash stuff. Every bottle that gets recycled is one bottle not going into the landfill. Thanks for doing your part! Plus, it is absolutely required as part of your initiation into the Casual Conservation Corps. Now drop and give me 20!

*Can I **re-ward** my kids for knowing what to do with this stuff?* If you think some *thing* has another use but you just can't come up with the solution, drop it in your kids' hands. They're smart and resourceful and they have the time! You will be surprised what comes out of the mouths of babes. Reward your children for keeping that some *thing* out of the landfill, air or ocean. Don't have kids? Put the neighborhood kids to work.

Will it look nice in my attic? Millions of Americans have filled their attics or basements to capacity and are now renting space in off-site storage units. This is great for the taxpayer, since these things are not filling up the landfill but not so good for your pocket book. Still, it is better to hold on to things than to trash them.

If there is nothing left to do and I trash it, will it go into landfill, air or ocean? Solid trash in the United States usually goes from your trash can to the landfill, where it gets buried beneath even more trash. This is definitely a better result than burning it into the air or sending it to the ocean. However, there are some drawbacks to landfills. With no air, it is impossible for buried trash to biodegrade. Plus landfills emit greenhouse gasses like CO^2 and methane. And it takes energy to drive it to the dump, something you pay for through your garbage bill, taxes or pocketbook.

Garbage that doesn't make it to our landfills often finds its way through our sewers to the ocean or other water sources. This includes toilet water, sink water and anything dropped into the neighborhood gutter where water flows. Cigarette butts often find their way to the sea because smokers drop them on the streets where they roll into the storm drain and into some water source. Sure, some of this waste is filtered but not all and heavy storms often overwhelm the filtration systems, sending raw sewage and your cigarette butts directly into a nearby water source. And from what I hear, we're in for some monster storms!

Lastly, and most importantly, some of our stuff is burned and finds its way into the air. You all know oil breaks down into bad stuff for our air but what about all the coal we burn to provide electricity to our homes? What about all the old tires we burn to provide that same electricity? This is necessary for keeping your home lit and heated but not good for the planet.

These last three methods – landfill, ocean or air – might seem like an energy-efficient way of waste disposal. Gravity pulls water down the gutters to the ocean, the mothering air magically cloaks the smoke and fumes in her warming embrace and Earl the Garbage Dude up-shifts from 8th to 9th gear hauling your stuff to the graveyard of stuff. No muss, no fuss! And as long as it doesn't inconvenience us by raising air temperatures or ruining a day at the beach, there is little cost to us...personally.

This seems like a good time to talk about the scientific community and their consensus on global warming. The Intergovernmental Panel on Climate Change (IPCC), a consensus of scientists, stated in its April 2007 report on climate change that "it is likely that anthropogenic (human caused) warming has had a discernible influence on many physical and biological systems." First off, the IPCC is a partnership between the World Meteorological Organization (WMO) and the United Nations Environment Programme (UNEP). It is the IPCC's job to evaluate other people's research "relevant to understanding the scientific basis of risk of human-induced climate change." It is also the IPCC's job to identify potential future impacts and to offer solutions. When the IPCC says it is 'likely' humans are contributing to climate change, they quantify that as a 66 to 90% probability. Given these odds, what does the gambler do?

A few people are not so sure humans are contributing to warming temperatures. I recently attended a global warming discussion and was surprised to hear dissent in the audience. When I got outside, I was met by a few non-scientists curbside but I stopped to listen to what these people had to say on the matter anyway. They talked of scientific fraud, cooked statistics and misleading information. Not being an expert on the matter, I was in no position to argue with them. If you wish to explore this debate further, key word 'global warming debate' into your favorite search engine.

But it occurred to me that this is not some insignificant debate. The stakes are high for both the environment and the economy. Suppose we were parents at home waiting for our children to return from school or basketball practice but they were late. Would we continue to pay our bills and hope they make it home okay? Or would we make sure they were safe by text messaging them, calling their friends or going outside to look for them? I see little difference between concern for our children and concern for the environment. They are inextricably intertwined and important to each other.

Given the odds that humans *are* causing climate change, what does a father or mother do? They bet on their children. Besides, if all those scientists at the IPCC are wrong, the damage is small compared to the damage if they are right. So you can bet that global warming is a hoax and if you are wrong, your children are in big trouble. Or you can bet that Man is causing climate change and if you are wrong, Al Gore is buying a round of drinks for everyone. Well, I don't know that for sure but that's the word on the street.

Given all the scary statistics related to global warming, I would give up hope. But I have to live here. There is nowhere else to go except the International Space Station which holds maybe 80 to 90 people, standing room only? And who wants to hang out in space boredom for several decades with the same people, waiting for the earth to cool down!? So there's no going back. We need to change course, to tack in sailing terms, to avoid one possible future...one that is increasingly becoming more probable. Ever tried to reverse an accelerating train? The same principle applies here – it takes time and every minute of delay requires two more minutes to stop. Add to that the side effects of trying to stop this train quickly, like spilled coffee and crying babies, and you begin to understand why you need to START TODAY. And for those of you who think we are too far gone, that the end is near, that it is all over but the crying, I say to you, "It ain't over till we say it is!"

STAGE 4
The Goods (At Home)

CHAPTER 1: WHAT A WASTE...

> "To waste, to destroy, our natural resources, to skin and exhaust the land instead of using it so as to increase its usefulness, will result in undermining in the days of our children the very prosperity which we ought by right to hand down to them amplified and developed."
>
> *–Big Papa Bear President Theodore "Teddy" Roosevelt, Jr., in his seventh State of the Union address, December 3, 1907*

The facts: Americans send 245 million tons of municipal solid waste to landfills each year or 4.5 lbs. of garbage per American per day.[4] Each ton, pound and ounce of waste you can keep out of your local landfill benefits the environment, and ultimately, your bottom line. How? In addition to reducing the costs of producing, collecting/maintaining, and purchasing the land to store this waste, your waste reduction efforts will conserve energy, materials and decrease greenhouse emissions like carbon dioxide and methane gas. Truth is, much of this garbage can be recycled, composted, reused, or even refused. Certain plastic containers, cans and paper are acceptable for reconstitution by those good people at the waste management company and there are pick up programs in many communities. You don't have one in yours? Hound your government leaders until they file a restraining order. Hey, it's their job to organize stuff like this for you! Do you work for them or do they work for you?

Every time I go to the grocery store, I bring home ten new bags. What should I do with them?

Bag-Packs

Lesson: We all know we should reuse those plastic and paper bags we get from the market. However, my biggest problem is that these bags are never where I am when I need them. You can create to-go Bag-Packs by stuffing one bag into another and compressing the whole lot with a rubber band so that it becomes really, really small. Then you can drop five in the car trunk, two in dad's briefcase, one in mom's purse, one in Rover's collar, one in your neighbor's hands and the rest in a kitchen drawer at home. Bag-Packs also make thoughtful and useful gifts. Trade one with the postman in exchange for those coveted wide rubber bands she always carries with her.

Lesson: These Bag-Packs are especially handy when you are out on walk-about and cannot find a place to recycle those cans and bottles. Simply, tie a bag to a nearby trash can and drop your recyclables inside. The homeless or the trash entrepreneurs will see to it those bottles get recycled. This is a form of just-in-time conservation!

Dogs Rule

Lesson: In Northern California, good people tie their grocery bags to trash cans in the parks and on the beach, where the free dogs roam. This makes scoopin' the poop in so much easier when there is a bag nearby.

Rant: Note to dog owners who think poop is some kind of sidewalk art: your days are numbered. Unfortunately, they never try to escape justice in front of me. This burns me so. I hate the fact I have to walk around town scanning the ground for land mines when I would rather be greeting my neighbors and meeting girls. It would be SO beautiful to catch a scatlaw in the act – kind of like catching some scofflaw in the act of keying your car. What would you do? If I caught some scatlaw leaving her dog's business for someone else to step on, I would grab one of my bag-packs and do the job for her. Then I would deposit my treasure on her doorstep – preferably in a blind spot she won't see on her way to work in the morning. But that's just me.

My biggest recycling challenge is getting the recyclables from the kitchen to the garage where the recycle bin rests. It's a long walk and I am busy-lazy.

Recycle Big and Loud

Lesson: Purchase a good-looking recycling tub BIGGER THAN your kitchen garbage can and place it on the kitchen floor for all the kids to see. This way, there can be no excuses for laziness. A nice looking basket can be purchased on the cheap from your local thrift store. Go there with your kids and help them pick out a winner, just as you would pick a plump pumpkin in October or a towering tree in December or a plucky pound puppy anytime.

Lesson: Challenge your kids to decorate the basket and be proud to display their artwork at dinner parties. Your friends will be totally impressed while your kids will look like angels, instead of the little devils you know them to be.

Lesson: Make sure to drop in only those items acceptable to your local recycler. How do you know what is acceptable? The garaged bin should have instructions on the lid. Instructions can also be found by submitting the keywords 'recycle' and '<your county>' into your favorite search engine. Print these instructions out and fasten it to the side of the basket. Easy smeasy! What, no Internet access? Go to the local library, Internet café or ask a neighbor. Make sure to bake your neighbor a pie in return for the favor. This will ensure future Internet access.

Lesson: Challenge your kids to fill the recycle bin faster than the garbage pail. I now make more trips to the recycle bin than I do the garbage can. Make sure to clean your recyclables thoroughly so they don't raise a stink. Do this with used dish water and you get bonus points. Prior to taking the indoor garbage to the outdoor garbage bins, make a second sweep for recyclables through all the garbage pails. It may be sticky, stanky work but who knows, you may discover that Ed McMahon actually delivered that $10M check but was too busy to present an oversized copy in person.

Some of my family's waste, like plastic bags and milk cartons, cannot be recycled. What to do?

Throw 'em in the neighbor's back yard! No, no, don't do that unless you like Black Sabbath blasted at your bedroom window in the wee hours of the morn.

Lesson: Plastic is made from oil-based chemicals and other stuff. In a sense, plastic is oil. It is a by-product of the oil refining process. Most plastic bags are made of Low Density Polyethylene, a plastic formula that rocketed up the charts to #4 on the resin identification coding system created by The Plastic Bottle Institute of the Society of the Plastics Industry (PBISPI). The PBISPI (pronounced *pub-spy*) are the guys who created those familiar triple chasing arrows encircling the number you see on plastic bottles. It's a little known fact that if you stare at those arrows long enough, you can see Elvis, or the Virgin Mary. I can't remember which.

Paper versus Plastic

Rant: The hottest water cooler debate of our time is about which shopping bag material is better for the planet: paper or plastic?

Paper has an old-timey feel to it and can be composted as long as there is not too much ink on the outside. However, it is unlikely paper will biodegrade when buried under a foot of landfill trash where there is no oxygen or sunlight to jumpstart the process. Paper is born of a renewable energy source. That means that as long as we are replacing the same number of trees that we harvest from the forests, there should be enough trees to make paper bags forever. However, I believe that trees are declining in large numbers across the world so I don't know how accurate it is to call the tree a renewable resource when it's not actually being renewed. If they all fall to logging, clear-cutting, forest fires and pestilence, there won't be any trees left to use. Just ask the Lorax.

On the other hand, Plastic, which comes from oil, is not a renewable energy source. There is only so much oil contained in the ground. Plus, plastic takes like a bazillion years to biodegrade. And there is always the fact that America is heavily dependent on foreign oil. Also, supermarkets tend to double-bag groceries so the bags don't break. Do they really need to do that? However, plastic also has some redeeming qualities. It is created as a by-product of the oil refining process and, therefore, is a type of oil reuse. Plastic bags are smaller and lighter than paper bags and take up a lot less space in the landfill. Plastic bags perform better when wet and use a lot less energy to create *and* recycle.

And when you use less energy to create and recycle something, you create less greenhouse gasses. Wait, this is an important concept. How is a paper or plastic bag created? A manufacturing plant burns coal, natural gas or oil and uses water to cool their machines to create the energy needed to transform trees and oil into bags. And what happens when natural resources are burned to produce energy? You guessed it – greenhouse gasses happen.

So for me, I slightly lean towards plastic bags in this debate because they add fewer greenhouse gasses to the atmosphere *today.* Plus, paper bags take away trees which absorb carbon dioxide, one of the greenhouse gasses. So when a paper bag is made, it not only releases greenhouse gasses into the air, it reduces the earth's ability to reabsorb those gasses. However, I don't think choosing either paper or plastic is a bad decision. A better decision is to reuse your paper or plastic bag again and again and again.

There are a whole bunch of other arguments in the plastic versus paper fight. Some people argue in favor of canvas bags made of cotton, hemp or some other renewable farming resource. However, there's way too much information to cover the entire debate in this little book. If you would like a good starting point, please keyword 'paper or plastic' into your favorite search engine. Of course, any reused bag kicks a recycled bag's butt in a PBISPI-endorsed kick bagging match. Let's get ready to rustle!

It's a little strange that while most recycling programs accept paper, few accept plastic bags. In the year 2000 of these United States of America, 20% of paper bags were recycled while only one percent of plastic bags were recycled[5]. Why is this?

Reuse is the most efficient way of stemming the flow of plastic bags to our landfills, parking lots and oceans. Plus, it is not always clear cut that those bags are actually being recycled and not being thrown into the landfill. I have heard news reports of huge truck-sized bales of plastic bags, intended for recycling, being dumped into landfills and people's back yards. In Christchurch, New Zealand they practice 'Real Recycling' which means the recycling companies take only what they can recycle and actually recycle what they take. This means that Kiwi consumers must take ultimate responsibility for their waste. This is just like when you're sitting at the dinner table and mum tells you to eat all you want, but take only what you're gonna eat. Mum knows best.

The Considerate Kitchen

Lesson: Cut your napkins in half! If you must use roll-cast paper towels as napkins, cut them up into two- or four-squares. The packaging said 'super absorbent', right? This works especially well when you are at the coffee house or restaurant cuz other people see you doing it.

Lesson: Find a way to finish each meal using one napkin only, unless of course you're eating barbecue ribs. Mmmmmmm! Brothers' Ribs!

Lesson: Mop up spills with an old sponge, not a legion of paper towels. Tell the kids Sponge Sally needs a bath and put them to work.

Feeling Pickled

Lesson: Soup cans and pickle jars are my favorite types of waste cuz in most cases you can both recycle and reuse them. Pickle jars make great pencil holders, coin banks or future pickling containers. Ever tried to pickle your own vegetables? Add water, salt, oil, vinegar, vegetables and voila! It's a little more involved than that so check the Internet for recipes. And a homemade pickled vegetable jar makes a great gift! Soup cans become storage containers for nails, screws and rubber bands to be used in the construction of the Bag-Packs. Soup cans and a string make a great alternative to cell phones, should the Stone Age ever return.

How about your beloved deceased dog's remains? Uhh, you may want a more secure container. Be sure to clean those jars and cans thoroughly first or you might receive some unwanted visitors like ants or Rover's ghost.

Lesson: Reuse as many containers as possible. I use my glass juice bottles as tap water bottles, my jammy jam jars for beer drinking and my beer bottles as flower vases. What an identity crisis! In fact, I use all sorts of containers for flower vases – beer/liquor/wine bottles, pasta jars and spinach cans.

If I find a really funky shaped bottle with a cool label, I rinse it and take it with me to the flower shop where I ask them to cut some flowers to fit my bottle. Then I throw on a bow, cuz research shows woman are 30% less likely to break the bottle over your head if there is a bow tied to it. For around $5 or $10, you conserve resources and totally start the evening off on the right footprint. If she's the right kind of girl, she'll appreciate your efforts to save the planet for your future grandchildren. Women – guys don't like to admit it, but we like getting flowers every once in a while, especially flowers that come in our favorite beer bottle. This is especially effective when you give it to us while we're watching sports with the boys. Oh, the jealousy! As for Mongo, a woman who gives him a yellow rose rose in a bottle of Blue Moon will definitely get him howling.

That's all great but you're not really saving me any money. I thought this book was about saving money!

Mongo: Actually, I am saving you money come property tax time when you don't have to contribute to a new landfill. But that isn't very sexy now, is it? I would like to tell you that wasting less will lower your monthly garbage bill but that isn't true in most towns and cities. Why don't you take the initiative? Rally your neighbors and lobby the city or county that contracts with the waste disposal company. Ask them nicely to charge you less for tossing less garbage. If that doesn't do the trick, then ask STRONG and LOUD. Residents in cities like Santa Cruz, California and Portland, Oregon have more money in their pockets because they already do this. Check out the "Pay as You Throw" program sponsored by the U.S. government.[6]

Lesson: You can save money another way. A friend of a friend takes her glass jars to the market to fill them with bulk foods. This is typically cheaper than buying prepackaged food in a plastic container. She labels her jars so she knows when she's running low on granola or rice. Plus, her kitchen pantry looks like a spice-rack of bulk foods – it is easier to find what she is looking for.

Garden Goodies

Lesson: Learn to compost and build a beautiful garden. Green thumbs tell me that you can avoid the garbage disposal and garbage pail for most food items. You save money because you don't have to buy as much fertilizer, you waste less water and avoid your landfill. And while food is bio-degradable, it is highly debatable how well this works buried under 10 tons of garbage without any air to jumpstart the process. Most importantly though, your garden looks marvelous (do that Billy Crystal thing)! What do I do? Check out www.HowToConserve.com[7] for a link to a government web site on composting. Hey, you already paid for this web site so you might as well use it!

CHAPTER 2: WATER, WATER EVERYWHERE

The facts: We can't live without water. Americans consume over 345 billion gallons of fresh water or 1,210 gallons per American per day[8]. This figure includes fresh water used to: irrigate the food you eat, power the thermo-electric energy plant that provides the electricity you use, cool the machines that produce the car you drive and clothes you wear, and water your garden and thirst. Isn't it funny how everything we do is interconnected? When you drive your car less, use less electricity at home or ski naked, you are saving water!

Compare this with the consumption levels of people in dryer climates such as Africa (195 gallons/African/day)[9] and you begin to understand what 'Land of Plenty' really means! Reducing your water consumption at home cuts down not only on your water bill but can reduce your sewage bill as well, or at least that portion of your tax bill attributed to sewer expenses. And when a drought returns, and it always does, communities with water conservation on the brain will be more adaptable and less likely to need high-cost water subsidies from other sources. Don't become a victim of Agua Darwinism!

My town has plenty of water this year so I drench my lawn, wash my car regularly and run headfirst down the kid's slip 'n slide. Nobody seems to mind this year. But I'm worried there might not be enough water in future years.

Mongo: "Yep, you can't live without water. You're lucky to have clean water flowing from a tap. Many people in the world drink bad water, water that keeps them alive but kills them slowly and disables them with disease. But they drink it anyway cuz nothing else matters if you ain't got water. Global warming may upset the cycles of your water supply. Some areas will get more rain, while others less. Since we don't really know how it is all going to turn out, you might as well prepare and train yourself for drought and pray to the water god to keep you flush. **Prepare, train and pray**. Hope for the best but prepare for the worst, I always say."

More Garden Goodies

Lesson: Collect rain water. It may require a little work, but you could shave off a few feet of your home's rain gutter at the nose, where the water flows out onto the ground, and drop a bucket underneath. Save that water by affixing a lid to the bucket and storing it in your garage or near the house while you wait for drier times. This water will most likely have dirt and leaves in it and so will be perfect for gardening. However, in a pinch, this water can be filtered and drunk.

Lesson: Set the timer to run your lawn and garden sprinklers at night or early morning so the water has a better chance of making it to the roots before the sun begins to vaporize your hard work and money.

Shower Time!

Lesson: Throw all the kids in the same bath. Make sure the water is not too hot first! Then take a cue from Henry Ford and run the assembly line!

Lesson: If you must shower instead of taking a bath, turn off the nozzle whenever soaping. This is a trick used by U.S. Marines in boot camp to save water and shorten shower time. Saving water saves lives, SIR! You can also attach a low flow nozzle purchased cheaply from your local hardware store. If you get lucky and share the shower with a partner, trade places when soaping instead of turning off the flow. Yabba!

Lesson: Use a smaller towel (hand-size) for drying off...you will save washing trips.

Lesson: When the shampoo runneth no more, use all the remaining sh'poo by adding some water to the mix. Sh-sh-sh-shake it! Then just squeeze the bottle till the juice runs over your head. I usually get five to ten more shampoos out of a bottle using this method. $$$

Lesson: Soap runs into our streams, lakes and bays through our drains so you may want to shampoo less frequently or use biodegradable shampoos that break down into healthier components for fish. Don't forget, your drain water goes into the ocean.

Back to the Basins

Lesson: Any shaving you need to do standing up can be done in a hot cup of water and not under a running tap. Same goes for the toothbrush. Folks who don't have central plumbing know all about this one.

Lesson: This isn't England! Your home may not have separate hot and cold water faucets where the hot water is ready and willing. Don't wait for the water to warm up when shaving...use cold water. It's brisk, baby! However, try to use a new razor since this is not ideal for the skin. If you must use hot water for shaving or washing your hands and face, drop a pitcher under the faucet to collect the cold water while you wait. My friend Mariko then uses the pitcher to water her plants or to make lemonade.

Lesson: Skip a day of shaving. Tell those smirks in the office that you are growing a beard or layering up for winter. Or tell them you mistakenly washed your face or legs with the boss' hair growth formula.

Lesson: By the way, if you run out of shaving cream, soap works nicely. Just lather up your face real good. I use this method when traveling so I don't have to fit a large shaving cream canister in my bathroom tote.

Lesson: When cleaning the bathroom, use old newspapers to wipe down mirrors after cleaning them. Done correctly, this will give you a clean, streak-free mirror. Then, apply shaving cream to an area of the mirror at face level and wipe away completely. Do not clean this area again. This will prevent that area from fogging up for a week or more, allowing men to shave immediately after showering when their pores are still open. Ladies, you can do whatever it is you ladies do in the privacy of your privy.

Eau de Toilet

Lesson: Don't flush after the first, or if you feel lucky, second trip to the bowl. If you leave the lid up to provide emergency H_2O for your dog or cat when you are away, flush before leaving or you could have a sick puppy on your hands.

Lesson: Try that with #two. On second thought, forget I said that. If it's yellow, let it mellow. If it's brown, flush it down.

Lesson: Place a few small, sealed, non-biodegradable, non-breakable containers in the water closet (WC) portion of the toilet. Plastic water bottles work great but I use beer bottles cuz I like to live dangerously. You can fool your john into thinking there's more water in the WC than there really is. So each flush actually uses less water! Just make sure you ain't the cloggin' kind because you weaken the flushing action of your commode when doing this. Fill the bottles with fresh water so you can drink them in an emergency. Make sure the containers are securely placed away from the flushing valve in the WC so it doesn't prop the valve open, causing the water to run. By the way, *in an emergency, the WC may contain your only source of fresh water.*

What's a water closet? The WC is the huge ceramic tombstone filled with fresh water just above the throne where you sit. Your toilet, commode, can, comfort station, head, john, latrine, potty, throne, sandbox, and porcelain bus is a wonder of modern technology. After doing your business, you flush the bus by depressing the handle, causing a whole stream of events to occur. The 'flushing' mechanism actually lifts a flush valve in the WC, releasing a torrent of fresh water down into the bowl and through a siphon jet that forces the bowl's inhabitants down the drain. It's actually a bit more complex than that but at least you now know how to turn your toilet into a conservation ally.

Dish it Up

Lesson: When washing dishes by hand, turn off the tap, tap, tap! Find the largest bowl or pot you need to wash, wash it thoroughly, fill it with hot water and soap, and then wash all other dishes from inside the Big Pot. Replace the dirty water as needed. Shoot, why not crank the radio and hand-wash everything?! You use less water than the dish washing machine, less electricity and you can hone those karaoke skills. I bet this is BIG in Japan.

Lesson: Instead of towels, use a drying rack for all hand-washed dishes. My old-timey apartment was built with this in mind. My kitchen cabinet shelves have Swiss-cheese holes in them which allow me to put away my wet dishes with the confidence that they will be dry in the morn. Of course, this only works if there is air blowing over those holes so I leave open the cabinet door. You could also try attaching all the dishes to your body and going for a run. This dries the dishes, provides your exercise for the day and ensures that the whole town stays the heck out of your way – a three-for-one deal!

Lesson: If you are more comfortable using the dishwasher, be sure to fill it completely before running it. Use the energy saver on your dishwasher. This lowers the temperature of the dry cycle and saves you moolah-la-la!

Lesson: Skip the dry cycle on the dishwater. When you hear that low hum that indicates the dishes are being dried, simply open up the dishwasher door and let evaporation happen naturally.

Lesson: Try not to use those flimsy, throw-away paper plates and silverware for your next party or picnic. This is Big Time wastefulness. The tougher plastic kinds can be washed and reused. Make sure everyone at the picnic knows to do this. Or borrow your neighbors' dishes for parties. You were going to invite them anyway, right?

Laundering the Green

Lesson: Run a full load of clothes each time you run the washer/dryer. If you have nothing to wear, dig deep in your closet. Your old look may not win you any awards but take solace in the fact that it was fashionable at one time, long, long ago. What, your closet is empty? Go to your local thrift store and make sure you always have a full load of clothes to wash.

Pit Check

Lesson: Okay, underwear should never be worn more than once a day, but how about re-wearing shirts and pants that haven't been to the gym? And while we're on the subject, who the heck cares how you look at the gym?! Thanks for letting me get that weight off my chest. Fewer trips to the washing machine mean less water and soap used and that's good for the fish, as well as your pocketbook. Just make sure you do a stain check on those pants and a pit check on those shirts. Except maybe in Bezerkely,

CA, there's nothing more embarrassing than being on a date where your scent is stronger than your game.

Lesson: If you have the time, break out that washboard, soap, the radio or karaoke machine and start strummin'. This saves water and energy. It is also an excellent workout. Note to self: cancel gym membership.

Rant: New Technology on the horizon! I recently read an AP article entitled, "What's that smell? Oh, It's the Police." Apparently, police in heat-stroking Ahmadabad, India are sweaty smelly. It's not their fault – they're out of doors all day in the hot sun directing traffic and keeping the peace. But hope is on the horizon for these odoriferous officers. The plan is for new uniforms using a light-weight, sweat-free scented new fabric. This funk-free fabric comes in soothing rose, tangy lemon and new car smell. Wow, this could reduce, or even eliminate, the need for washing machine visits. Sounds like a great idea to me as long is it isn't itchy-rashy-uncomfortable. We'll see.

Gray Waters

Lesson: Find alternative means to water your garden before you go for the hose. It can be a little work but you can collect water from a variety of sources including your shower, bath, and sinks. For details on how to add gray water to your water budget, check out www.HowToConserve.com.[12] This is especially important in dry, desert areas of the country like New Mexico or Arizona. If anyone knows how to squeeze water from a stone, it's those Diamondbacks!

Lesson: "Can I have a glass of water, Mom?!" My friend Darsie takes all the undrunk water glasses from the previous night and uses them to water plants or to water the dog and cat bowls.

Rant: Just as I was about ready to print this book, a water story came over the news feed that is worth noting. Three large areas of California had just been cut off from their main water source for seven to ten days! Seems the water pumps delivering Delta water were one of the sources killing local smelt fish populations, whose numbers had significantly declined. The other sources cited were fertilizer run-off and invasive fish species. So the pumps were turned off to give the smelt a fighting chance.

Residents in the Tri-Valley, the Peninsula and a county near Los Angeles didn't notice the water shut down because their local water districts were able to keep delivering water to customers from local reservoirs and lakes. But this story brings up a bigger issue – are our cities prepared to deal with more water shortages? I lived near the Tri-Valley for nearly 20 years and have never once heard of the water being shut off before! Most of the water in California goes to the farmers who feed America. So if we experience more water shortages, who do you think is going to lose water first – farmers or city residents? What is the alternative should we drink up our reservoirs? These are important issues and I will keep my eye on them.

CHAPTER 3: PAYING THE BILLS & OTHER PAPER CHASES

The facts: 213 billion pieces of mail are sent to homes and businesses every year.[13] That's a lot of greeting cards and bills!

Rant: But much of that flow – four million tons or 62 billion pieces – is junk mail you may not want[14]. That's 206 pieces of junk mail per American each year! Don't we all have enough junk in our lives – in our food, in our attics and in our trunks? If I see another postcard from a real estate agent I've never met who covers a part of the country I don't want to buy in, I think I'm going to scream. I have nothing against real estate agents, having been one myself, but as the teachers they are supposed to be, some of them might show a little more class. Of course, the reason they keep sending you those postcards is because 10% of you respond in some way and it only takes one real estate sale to more than justify the expense of sending out all those postcards.

Let Your Fingers Do the Walking

Lesson: Contact 1-888-5 OPT OUT (or 1-888-567-8688) to reduce the junk being mailed to you by the major credit agencies and their minions. There is no central source for axing all junk mail but you significantly reduce the volume by contacting the major offenders.

Lesson: When you recycle those envelopes sent by your creditors and junk mail dogs, make sure to tear out the plastic film that covers the address opening. Make sure you recycle ONLY those items identified by the recycling company. If you don't, the entire batch of recycling (you and all your neighbor's recycling) may be considered contaminated which means it's off to landfill prison for everybody!

Lesson: Just shred it! Invest in a shredder ($20-$30) at your local office supply store or buy a pair of scissors at the local dollar store. For a small investment, you can create party confetti or a paper wig, two good paper reuses. You get the added benefit of decreasing your chances of becoming a victim of identity theft. Americans throw away 27 billion pieces of junk mail every year without opening them.[16] Identity thieves just love to root through your garbage looking for information they can use to drive down your credit rating while accumulating more stuff for *their* local landfills! And the time and dollar cost of repairing your credit can be huge and will involve reams of paperwork to sort out. This is a totally frustrating downturn in your life – worse than getting a speeding ticket but probably better than being diagnosed with a life threatening disease. If you have had your identity stolen and are finally clear of the damage, just let it go. Learning to brush off the wrongs of others is a major step in reclaiming your identity.

Lesson: Switch to online bill paying and save paper. At the time I wrote this lesson, I had not set up online bill paying for my own personal finances. I hesitated for years because I feared the Internet. I felt naked. They wanted me to expose all sorts of personal information like social security number, birth date and favorite ice cream that are the keys to identity theft. And for all their trumpeting about security, banks are still successfully attacked by hackers and thieves who grab the personal account information of millions of satisfied customers. Of course, the banks are quick to repair the damage and I'm sure they are adapting to the challenges of the online world. As I prepared for my book tour, I realized I had to make a choice – either bank online or hire an accountant to pay my bills for me. When you see me coming down the road, ask me what I did.

The Paperless Office

Rant: Once upon a time, I worked in an office where we provided shelter for reams and reams of snowy, white paper so we could imprint our wisdom on them. After telling our stories, we would kiss our reams goodnight and lay them lovingly in large, warm beds called file cabinets. There they would sleep for days, months and years, dreaming of crazy-eyed squirrels and warm maple syrup. And whenever we needed to awaken these reams from their dreams, we would have to get up from our desks to find their sleeping spot which could take five to fifteen minutes, depending on donuts. Management – think about all that lost productivity! Worker bees – think about all those yummy, icing-covered pastries! This was only five years ago. Today, five years later, my old office still has the same number of file cabinets it did back then. Bravo! Not only did they cut down on paper use but raised productivity by actually using something called a C...O...M...P...U...T...E...R. Sure we had computers five years ago but, like I was saying earlier, lifestyles are particularly difficult habits to break. Didn't you get the memo?

Nose Mud

Lesson: If your recycling center accepts tissues (mine does not), drop those little boogers in the bin. That's another reason you got the bin lidded. If not, make sure they make it to the trash can. I hate seeing snot rags on the street. Don't you?

Lesson: Buy a cotton cloth hanky, add some panky and blow. It won't take up too much extra room in the washing machine and, if you add a monogram, you will look suave and debonair while you are squeezing the goose. Guys, if you wear a suit, always keep a clean handkerchief in your breast pocket – it's not for you but for the lady if she should ever cry or have a little noticeable nose mud.

Rant: To all the sleeve wipers, grow up. To all the gold miners, keep it up. You people seem to think you are invisible when you are driving your cars, but you're actually the greatest show on earth! And for this I am soooo grateful. I could be having the worst day of my life, "dog died, girlfriend left me and, oh yeah, saw some dude digging for gold...digging deep! Fifty bucks says he eats it!" I wonder what goes through their heads as they zip down the road? *La la la. I think I'm alone now, doesn't seem to be anyone around.*

CHAPTER 4: ENERGY DRUNK

The facts: 15% of the energy consumed in America is in the house[17]. It's also where we use the greatest number of electrical and natural gas appliances. There's television sets, refrigerators, microwaves, stereos, computers, cell phones, foot massagers, overhead lighting, lamps, heaters, air conditioners, hot water heaters, and on and on and on and on. This makes it harder to save energy because it must be done one appliance at a time. But you have a great incentive to take the time – money! American households spend $109 billion, or $378 per person per year on energy in our homes.[18] For a family of four, average energy bills can be $1200 per year! But there are a few ways you can put some green back in your wallet, as well as back in the earth.

Air raid!

Lesson: In the winter, turn your central heat down each night to 65 degrees F, or lower if you wish. You may want to install radiator heaters in occupied bedrooms so you're not heating the entire house while you sleep or you could pile on the blankets. Play with the formula a bit by lowering the temp a little more each night and see how it affects your comfort level, both physical and financial. Husbands and wives might consider sleeping nekid in order to warm up the marital bed quicker and share some warmth. Warning: this could lead to more kids.

Lesson: During the warm season, turn up your air conditioning (AC) to 70 degrees F, or higher at night, and install fans in the bedrooms or open the windows. Again, play with the formula till you are comfortable. However, there is no substitute for getting a good night's sleep. Don't cheat your sleep.

Lesson: Only blow heat or AC into the room you are occupying. First, close the registers, or air vents, in every room you are not in, except for the room containing the thermometer – that do-hicky on the wall that turns the air on or off. If you foolishly fool the thermometer into thinking it's colder than it really is in your room, then it will continue to blast you with heat and you will soon find life mighty uncomfortable. But if the thermostat reads the same temperature as your room, you should be able to find comfort. Closing every door in the house will also help retain heat throughout the house.

Lesson: Make sure you apply caulk to all your window frames and keep your drapes closed at night, unless you have the windows open for a draft. The windowpanes and frames are the biggest energy thieves in the winter and summer.

Lesson: If you have a maniacal, brainiacal child who is really into science, put her to work. Child labor laws are pretty outdated anyway, if you ask me. Challenge her to learn about the house's air system and find ways to reduce energy use and costs. Split the utility savings with her to make it a bit more interesting and *rewarding*. It's not a bribe – it's an allowance for allowing you to save money.

Power Down

Lesson: During the year, replace all burned-out incandescent light bulbs with fluorescent bulbs. These last longer and use significantly less energy. A lot of people choose to replace all their bulbs right away and they probably save more money than you in the long run. But if you don't have the money to replace them all now, don't beat yourself up. Replace bulbs as necessary. Some big-box stores will sell them in eight-packs for about $1 a bulb.

Lesson: If you own your home or building, solar panels have started to make more sense, especially since many utility providers provide a rebate on your purchase. Too much money to spend all at once? Some manufacturers and banks will even finance your purchase. If your house gets enough sunlight, this can be a good investment. However, not all solar panels or home locations are created equally. Do the math before investing.

You can guesstimate your annual rate of return using this formula: Investment Rate of Return = (Savings - Financing Costs) ÷ Whip-Out Money

Savings or expected total $$ saved per year is another formula that takes into account the number of days during the year that the sun is expected to say hello, expected annual utility costs if you don't buy solar panels, tax savings or utility rebates and the efficiency rate of the particular solar panels you wish to buy. These are the main items you need to consider – there are other considerations to add to the recipe. This number is more art than science so get help. When the solar guy tells you your purchase will return 3% on your money, ask him to explain, in detail, how he arrived at this figure, number by number. Check those figures with other solar guys and gals or on the Internet to see if his information seems logical.

Financing Costs are the yearly loan payments you make to the bank or lender who actually paid for the solar panels. You usually make these payments on a monthly basis so total up the 12 months of payments to get this figure. Do not include your down payment or any other wad of cash you have to whip out when you purchase your solar panels.

Whip-Out Money is the one-time wad of cash you hand over to the manufacturer and/or bank. Sometime it is called a down payment. Whatever the bank or solar panel manufacturer calls it, it is any cash that leaves your wallet at the time of purchase. Do not include future monthly financing costs in this figure.

Now you have a general idea of how much money your Whip-Out Money will make when you go solar. Is it 2%, 4% or 8% per year? How do you know if this is a good deal? If your decision to purchase is based solely on saving money, then compare this return on investment with other investments you could buy with your Whip-Out money including a savings account, certificates of deposit or real estate. Again, this is more art than science. Results may vary widely. While I believe this information to be correct, I make no warranties, expressed or implied, as to the accuracy of this information. Solar panel buyers should conduct their own independent investigations and rely solely and solarly on those results.

Speaking of warranties, many solar panel manufacturers will provide a warranty, some up to 20 years. Make sure the warranty is transferable to a new owner should you decide to sell your home. Make sure the next owner can transfer it should they decide to sell the house. Make sure your real estate agent trumpets these benefits in their marketing materials. Make sure the manufacturer is reputable and is likely to be around in 20 years to fix your panels should they break. Make sure you are a buyer who bewares. Caveat emptor. Make sure.

Trip the Lights

Lesson: Turn off the lights in unoccupied rooms. Add it to your children's list of chores. You already do this, right?

Lesson: Replace light switch panels with hybrid motion detection panels so your lights automatically go when you do. Don't worry, you can buy the panels that have a manual mode so they don't trip the lights when you are still, stalemated in a staring contest.

Lesson: Unplug electrical devices when not using. Even when your microwave is at rest, it still burns electricity. You have plenty of other ways to tell the time.

CHAPTER 5: THE GIFT ECONOMY

Lesson: Buy your gifts at the thrifts. These places are a pirate's treasure chest: T-shirts, vinyl records, stereo amplifiers, kitchenware, kid's toys and clothing, golf clubs, etc. Oh, your friends will call you cheap if you *gift thrift*? The way I look at it, that cool 'Vote for Pedro' shirt I recently bought only cost me $1.99 but I spent at least twenty minutes sorting through the t-shirt racks to find it, plus five minutes purchasing time, plus twenty minutes driving time and fuel expense. If my time is worth $20 per hour, that Pedro shirt actually cost me $19.99. Uh, I believe a 'thank you' is in order.

Long Rant: It has given me such mixed feelings over the years – do I show my friends I love them by giving them some *thing* or by freeing us both from the vicious cycle of holiday gift giving and holiday poverty? This issue gave me such headaches that in December 2003, I wrote the first draft of this book with the intention of gifting it to all my friends and relatives in lieu of 'real' gifts. This was the Great Compromise! I would spread the gospel on conservation while providing that physical *something* to my friends. And of course, there was no need for a card – each book would receive a personalized inscription from the actual author. But you already know the rest of the story.

In most of the cases it was hugely successful because it gave me and my friends something to talk about all year long. However, there was one glaring exception to this carousal of cheers: my girlfriend! Oh man, was my now-ex-girlfriend unhappy! And I crashed and burned for the heresy of the incident. What did I do wrong? I gave the one person in my life, who was supposed to be more special than anyone else, a copy of a book I gave out to 19 other people! Surely I must have still been dizzy from the alien abduction to make this obvious mistake.

So, molded by fire, I had to start evolving while the holidays kept revolving – Christmas, Valentines Day, a Birthday, Easter, Fourth of July, another Birthday, Halloween, Thanksgiving and finally Christmas again. Gadzoooks! The conveyor-belt gift idea that led to my first book would have been the perfect solution, except that now it seemed old and contrite. How could I get more creative?

I decided to *stop* giving stuff to everyone for every holiday and see what would happen. What happened is that, little-by-little, my friends stopped giving me stuff. What joy this brought the Grinch! A few of my more intuitive friends guessed at what I was up to and started gifting me services like massage and psychological counseling. But the point is that they still remained my friends! Sure, I lost a few friends but the ones who kept inviting me out for bowling were just the most amazing people! I am a lucky, lucky man. Drinks are on me.

And so my gift giving evolved once again. I felt compelled to let my friends know how much I appreciated their thoughtlessness, their lack of gifts. Instead of giving on national holidays, I decided to give *when I found some thing or some service worth giving.* I studied my friends and tried to get in their minds. What would make them laugh or jump up-and-down like Tom Cruise on a couch with joy? What could they really use?

This made gifting a little tougher. I would have to work harder at finding the right gift and I'm lazy-busy! But since I was no longer tethered to the whole national holiday system, there was no urgency. There was none of that 11th hour panic that convinces you to buy ceramic rabbits or beef jerky from the local mini mart. I could walk into a store I found interesting and walk right back out the door with empty hands. It was just that simple! I could take advantage of the *real* sales when they occurred after the holidays. I could shop anytime, anywhere.

And so life has become one constant shopping spree for me. Instead of going on gift trips, I look for gifts anywhere and everywhere I find myself, not just in the stores and malls. I am willing to buy new as easily as buying reused. I re-gift cool and useful stuff that I have no room for anymore in my apartment.

I go to garage sales. There is a reason why there's always at least one person who arrives early for the starting gun of a garage sale—you find amazing things at garage sales. I once picked up a $15 wood-shafted Calloway sand-wedge, perfectly weighted to get me off the beach and in the hole in two.

Even more amazing things can be found at thrift and second-hand stores. Most recently, I bought a beautiful formal raincoat at a Mormon thrift store in Idaho Falls, ID for $18.50! I still haven't found the friend who wears suits and shares my jacket measurements but I'll keep looking. Meanwhile, I will keep testing the raincoat out for that future friend.

I even take advantage of the cool stuff people leave on the streets by fixing them up and re-gifting. I found a box containing a pair of style-E sunglasses and a woman's handcrafted mask suitable for a formal Masquerade Ball, complete with rhinestones and a peacock's feather. That too is sitting in my apartment, fixed up, waiting for the right time and the right girl-friend.

So in conclusion, it is okay to miss holidays. *But how do I show the ones I love that I care?* It is okay to re-gift your stuff. It is okay to re-gift other people's stuff. It is okay to gift services. It is even okay to gift new stuff if you find that to be more comfortable. There is no judgment here. I will love you any which way you choose to display your gifting gratitude, as long as you observe The Way of the Casual Conservationist.

This seems to be the appropriate time to address the concerns of gift-driven retailers, the companies that supply them and the worker bees who keep them buzzing. "If people buy less new stuff, what will happen to us?" I won't blow smoke...if this attitude, this lifestyle choice ever catches fire, you are looking at fewer sales of your existing product lines and, quite possibly an unprofitable business model. Given human nature, you probably have nothing to worry about.

But if there was cause for concern, you don't have to just sit there and watch the train wreck happening. Why not offer your customers a 'returns' section so they can buy second-hand if they wish? Why not offer services that relate to your theme? If you are a cooking retailer, why not contract local chefs to do private parties or have in-store parties? If you sell books, why not offer guided tours of the city? If you sell bath products, why not offer a shower valet service to do the soaping and drying?

I know why not. Besides the obvious zoning hurdles you would face, it's harder to predict the outcome or maintain the quality of a service you don't perform yourself. Products are safe and sure. There is quality control – you know what you are going to get every time you unwrap this thing. Brand recognition is about guaranteeing performance. That is why McDonalds has been so successful – wherever you go in the world, you can count on the same yummy cheeseburger at a decent price. McDonalds gets a bad rap cuz people like guarantees and some people exercise the Micky D's guarantee a little too often, to the detriment of their hearts and waistlines. As for me, I like a hamburger and a liter of cola every once in a while. Sooooo good.

But I have faith in you, in your ability to adapt to a changing economic environment. Don't think of this new consumer attitude as an economic roadblock. Think of it as a challenge, a challenge to create new profit streams while saving our seas and streams. Get creative! Your shareholder's children and grandchildren are counting on you to protect their entire inheritance, and not just their money.

We now return to your regularly scheduled program. Rant off.

Wrap It Up

Lesson: Replacing store-bought wrapping paper with the daily newspaper will not earn you sneers and jeers. Your *real* friends will understand. If they're the sensitive-sort, use the Sunday comics and give them an added *guffaw*. Don't forget a reused bow or ribbon to add that thoughtful touch.

Lesson: Why wrap one gift when you can wrap two or more? Henry Ford had something when he introduced an assembly-line approach to making automobiles. By wrapping two or more gifts at the same time, you save time. Carpedium! Look for something in your house you like and wrap the carp! Now you have a ready-to-go gift for that last minute birthday party.

Gift Allies

Lesson: Form gift alliances with your friends that outline what form your presents shall take or if you should exchange gifts at all. For example, you agree to exchange only hand-made presents, online gift certificates or gifts without packaging. Cash is always nice. In fact, cash is the most thoughtful wedding gift for couples just getting started in this wild, wild world. Try it on nieces and nephews instead of pretending to know what's hip. Many Internet social networking sites offer 'gift requests' on your homepage so you can broadcast to the world your needs and wants.

CHAPTER 6: OTHER STUFF

Moving On Up

Lesson: Moving from place to place takes a lot of time and sweat, so it shouldn't also take up a lot of your green. Next time you need boxes for your move, take a drive down the back alley of your local supermarket or department store. I made one move entirely with the FREE boxes I found back there. Use duct tape to mend and support the boxes you find. Avoid boxes with food stuck to them. Gross!

Lesson: In my city, the retailers leave their cardboard boxes on their front porches for the cardboardmen to pick up. These guys are the coolest – one gave me a ride once when I couldn't find a taxi. They earn their livings by recycling my stuff! You see them driving down the street with cardboard stacked in their little trucks 10 stories high! I'm sure the cardboardmen wouldn't mind if you grabbed a box or two from the kerbside, as long as you returned them to a retailer's front porch near your new home.

Lesson: Many packaging stores will buy clean, well-endowed boxes for 25 to 45 cents per box and resell them to their customers. I've even seen some mobile services that will pick up/ drop off boxes at your home. How could moving get any easier or cost-effective?

Lesson: Use a couple of those boxes as nightstands or CD racks. If the sight of cardboard upsets your inner interior decorator, throw a nice scarf or tablecloth over the top. Don't forget to reinforce the boxes with duct tape. This is totally acceptable for anyone with no money to spend on furniture. There was a time when I did it. That time could come again.

Feel of the Cloth

Lesson: Social clothes can someday become garden clothes which can someday become wash rags...you get the point. DO NOT wash your car with old tidy-whities! I think the homeowner's association might prohibit that anyway.

Lesson: The local thrift store is never a bad ending for your wardrobe. Somebody who needs it more than you will reuse your clothing and it won't end up as waste. Plus, your donations are tax-deductible, in most cases.

Naïve Bottling

Rant: There is a big debate bubbling over still-water in a bottle. Some feel that the mountains of plastic bottles being produced and the long distribution routes needed to get them to you are an unnecessary waste of oil products when the tap water in most communities is clean and delicious. Others feel that bottled water is a necessary back-up in case local water supplies are ever contaminated or disrupted. Still others worry that the bottled water companies are diverting local, public water supplies from the people who need them most. Some people just like the convenience and security of bottled water when they are away from home. This is an interesting debate and an important one – one that grows in importance in times of drought.

Lesson: For now, the best thing to do is reuse your plastic water bottles. If your tap water stinks, call a water company that does home delivery. But DO NOT buy those pallets of water bottles...it's too easy to dismiss your current bottle when you know there are 200 fresh ones in the refrigerator. Since buying single bottles of water is relatively expensive compared to buying the 24-packs, you will have an incentive to keep your old bottle around and fill it with tap water. Label your bottles with a felt pen so each family member can identify their bottle in the refrigerator. For your health, buy new bottles occasionally and don't forget to recycle the old bottles. If you buy the few glass water bottles available, you can wash and reuse them indefinitely. If you want lots of quick, available bottled water, buy the huge five gallon containers with the spout and pour it into your used small bottles.

Lesson: I heard a story about this restaurant in Bezerkely, CA which had offered free bottled water to their customers. They could afford to do this because their price points were high, as was the quality of their food. But recently, they decided to stop serving bottles and to provide free tap water to their customers. What's so amazing about that? Instead of serving tap water still and chill, they bought a $400 carbonator to create bubbles. Brilliant! Restaurants with lower price points might consider charging 50 cents a glass until the Carbonator is paid off. Or they could mix syrups into the bubbly and make delicious drinks and charge more.

CHAPTER 7: THE HOME GAME

Conservation doesn't have to be a chore. Why not make it a game? The next few pages contain some of the images you saw in the previous chapters. I used these images to illustrate conservation lessons and now I am reusing these images as part of a fun game you can play with your kids. Even if you don't have kids, this game can help remind you to conserve resources right at the moment of maximum conservation opportunity. What is that? *The moment of maximum conservation opportunity* is that single moment when you are hovering over the sink with toothbrush in hand and you decide to either run the tap or to turn it off immediately after wetting your brush. It is that moment when you are about to leave a lit room and you decide to either walk straight out or stop to turn off the light. And yes, it is that moment when your hand is reaching for the flush handle on the toilet and you have the choice to let it mellow or flush it down! Each of these moments is a just-in-time conservation opportunity. But how do you remember to take advantage of these opportunities?

The Home Game is the Way. You start by cutting out all the do-it-yourself stickers that you are about to see at the end of this bonus chapter. Then you take a little scotch tape and turn them into real stickers! You stick them in areas around the house where your maximum conservation opportunities occur. Stick one on the mirror of your bathroom, one on the thermostat and one on your napkin holder. There is also a scorecard that you can tape to a common area in your home where everybody can see it. When you are done doing this, the game is afoot!

Each conservation opportunity that Bobby, Suzy or Dude performs successfully is worth a point. Then, it is their job to mark the scorecard. Everybody is on the honor system here so be honest! This is also a way to build trust between you and your kids. At the end of the week, tally the scores up and declare a winner! Depending on your views about competition, you may want to have a prize or a couple of prizes so all the kids feel included. Maybe you could make it a group effort to beat last week's total? A good prize might be a favorite dessert or some play time in the park with the 'rents. Whatever you decide, this is *your* Home Game so make it work for your family and above all, have fun with it.

After a few months, some of these stickers may get smelly-moldy-cruddy, so feel free to visit www.HowToConserve.com where you can print more FREE!

Here we go...

Save Paper Towels!

Fluorescent Bulbs!

Save One Flush?

Turn Off Tap!

Sleep Well!

Full Wash!

Full Wash!

Take Public Transportation!

Bag-Packs Here!

Save Water!

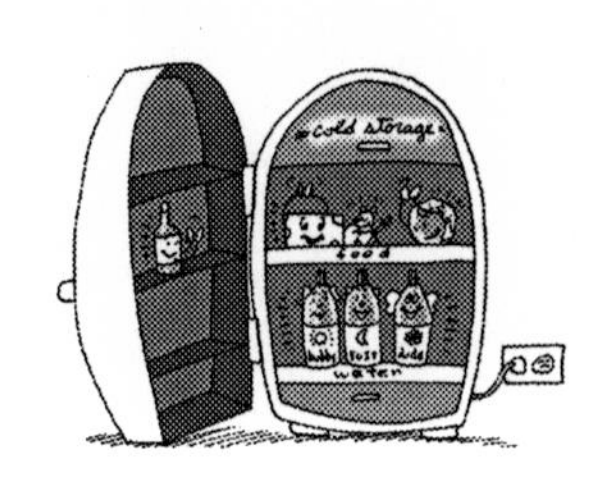

Reuse Water Bottles!

2-in-1 Napkins!

Recycle Here!

Shave In A Cup!

Turn Off Tap!

Turn Off Lights!

HOME GAME	Month:		Week:		Prize:			**TOTAL**
Name	MONDAY	TUESDAY	WEDNESDAY	THURSDAY	FRIDAY	SATURDAY	SUNDAY	
TOTAL								

Get more Home Game scorecards FREE at www.HowToConserve.com

STAGE 5
The Goods (On The Road)

CHAPTER 8: EATING OUT

This last year I began to notice how much trash I create when I'm on walkabout. Oftentimes, it was inconvenient to recycle the cans, bottles and paper cups I accumulated during the day. When I grabbed food to go, it came in several paper containers, plus napkins. The guilt drove me in another direction...

Lesson: If your local coffee shop doesn't provide recycling bins, leave cans and bottles on the rim of or next to the garbage receptacle. Even if no one comes by to recycle those cans and bottles, at least you are forcing the café owner and his/her employees to think about recycling and face their consciences.

Lesson: Keep ONE SACK (plastic, paper or canvas) in your car trunk or in your backpack for collecting your recyclables on the road. Leave no man behind. Or keep TWO SACKS, one for you and one for collecting the recyclables of the heretics. THREE SACKS may qualify you for sainthood.

Lesson: Ask for ceramic mugs and plates whenever possible. Take a minute to drink that coffee or eat that buttered muffin before starting your day. If you follow the Vince Lombardi code of arriving to all appointments 15 minutes early, you will have enough time to get to work.

Double-Cupped Coffee

Lesson: Some coffee shops offer a sleeve to keep your fingers from incinerating, while others give you two cups. Recycle the used inner cup, and save the outer cup and lid to be used later when you make coffee at home. Also makes great disposable cups for picnics.

Lesson: Bring your own coffee cup to the café. If you drink two cups a day like I do, you are saving up to 4 paper cups and 2 of those hand protector thingies every day!

Lesson: Choose your stores and coffee shops based on something other than convenience. Try it for one day and you will meet people you've never met before. As for me, I go for the little things...like their recycle-mindfulness or the beautiful barrista on the inside. Or I just dig the fat cuppa joe with that berry-delicious apricot scone. I especially go, go, go for the ready riposte of a barraging barista when I tell 'em my name is Inigo Montoya or Mongo or some such blather.

The Law of Conservation Probability

Rant: A company that makes one **significant** change in reducing the waste their product produces is much more likely to make more changes as they discover and afford them. These businesses should be applauded and patronized.

> Example: Brown Cow Yogurt of Antioch, California is my favorite active culture because they let you choose if you want to add the cream off the top or discard it for a lower-fat meal. And they produce and distribute their yogurt locally which means less drive time. Plus, they

just recently removed the plastic top from their yogurt cups in lieu of the aluminum foil top that was already there. Instead of removing the cap and the foil, now I just have the foil to remove. This saves time for me and saves the plastic-oil tree. Beautiful! What will Brown Cow think of next?

Lesson: There are two types of leftovers in this world my friends, those that can be doggy bagged and those that are just fine left in their shell. Consider the banana. The banana offers an appealing storage opportunity. Leave a half-eaten, half-peeled banana in the refrigerator for a day or so, remove the brown top and you've got a tasty afternoon pick me up. What other foods have self-contained storage opportunities?

Dining at Work

Lesson: If you go to a salad bar for lunch during the week and bring it back to your desk, bring a covered plastic container to use as your "plate". This may cost a teeny bit extra on the scale, unless the restaurant owner is a casual conservationist and gives you a modest discount – he's saving money anyway by not using his to-go plates. Keep silverware and mugs at work so you don't need to use the restaurant's disposable ones. Sneak into the company refrigerator and pour Patrick's soda into your mug. Poor Patrick, he should have hidden his beverage behind the week-old bagels!

Lesson: Vote with your pocketbook. Don't aide and abet the restaurateurs and java jockeys who only worship money, the bottom line and disposable packaging. Take your hard-earned dollars to the folks who worship something higher...like community, family and conservation. A little heavy, you say? Guess who's better to party with?!

Rant: It's kinda creepy these days...the way people are always forcing paper or plastic on you – at your grocer, department store, mini mart and donut shop. I am sure it's an alien invasion and they must be stopped! And we're just the ones to do it! Who's with me?

Lesson: Just say no to "paper or plastic?" except when you have run out of fingers to carry all your stuff. If you must sac, make sure you right-size. There's nothing more humiliating than carrying home a pack of gum in a mobile dog kennel. Bring your Bag-Packs with you. Bag-packs are the calling cards of the Casual Conservationist.

Lesson: Find a local grocer where you can refill your existing containers with new food. Don't do this with chicken and some other meats that can make you sick if you reuse their containers. But I see nothing wrong with liquid soap or granola.

Lesson: If you find yourself having ACCEPTED a bag to go but you change your mind, fold up the bag (if it is clean) and drop it in the hands of one of the worker bees – your gift to them and to this earth.

CHAPTER 9: OTHER STUFF

Smoke 'Em If You Got 'Em

Lesson: Smokers, did you know that it takes 10 years for the filter on your cigarette to decompose? Well, I don't know if that's really true – some people debate that it takes 1 year, while others say 20 years but it sure seems like there are a lot of butts hanging around everywhere I go. Some make it to the landfill where they have no chance to decompose, buried in an oxygen-deprived and sunless heap of trash. Others make it to the storm drain where they are washed out to sea so surfers and beach babies can enjoy them. And then there are the orphaned butts, the ones left in planter boxes and tree wells around town that are so beautiful to behold. The best place for butts? For now, make sure they make it to the landfill. Don't be a street butthead!

I don't smoke that often but sometimes I keep my filters in a cleaned-out spaghetti sauce jar or a mint box until I can figure out what to do with them. Maybe I'll use them someday in some artsy-fartsy sculpture. Got any ideas?

Lesson: Don't smoke around kids. The message you send to them is as dangerous as the second-hand smoke you massage into their lungs. A child develops imitating the actions of his parents, friends, anyone within visual or audio reach. Plus you're bigger than them and they look up to you...literally.

Rant: To the infants, toddlers, kids, and young adults: don't smoke. Hair will grow out of your ears and your fingernails will turn purple and fall off. No, not really. But I've heard the chances are good that it can stunt your growth. And if you think you are done growing, think again. I've had friends at 18-years-old gain a foot in height during their senior year in high school. They didn't smoke.

Trash Walks

Rant: Picking up trash on the street won't save you time or money, but it could save your sanity. Let me explain. I live in an amazing city. But all is not rosy on my streets. When I walk out my front door in the morning, the first thing I see is trash – discarded restaurant doggie bags, flyers, dog poop bags, live poop, candy bar wrappers, dry cleaning bags, newspaper pages, etc. It drives me crazy! But I keep my sanity by following one easy rule...

Lesson: Pick up one piece of trash per day. I try to do it in front of other people, especially children, in case they feel like imitating me. I always do it near a trash can so I don't have to carry it too far and I choose garbage that is relatively clean and dry. If you worry about germs, try carrying a bottle of waterless hand wash when venturing outside.

If you are pushing a baby stroller, it makes a nice vehicle for picking up multiple pieces of trash. My friend Adrienne and her daughter grab their gloves and plastic bags and go on walkabout in their neighborhood, competing for the most trash booty found.

Trash Hash

Lesson: When I was a wee tot, I ran a lot. Mostly I ran from bullies but that trained me for more challenging races like *The Hash.* The Hash is a race without an announced route or end point. The runners must find flour marks on the road that indicate a flour directional marker is near. The 'Trash Hash' uses the same concept except you must pick up trash along the way and load it into your backpack. We use the honor system so there is no rooting through trash-rich cans or dumpsters. It must be found on the ground. Each pound of trash cuts 10 seconds off your race time so the first over the line may not win the day.

If I say it's safe to surf this beach...

Rant: Anything you drop down a sewer drain or dump in a stream (even biodegradable materials) could be riding with you on that next tasty wave, bro. Unfortunately, some of our sewer effluent makes its way to the sea. There are filters in place but they don't catch everything. This is especially true during heavy rain storms when the filtering plants are overwhelmed with the volume of water so they release some water 100% unfiltered into the sea. The upside: The locals don't mess with sickly-looking, zombie surf jocks!

To those who poison our waters directly, just stop. To the shareholders of multi-national manufacturing companies who poison our waters, just stop. You've got a lot to lose here, and I don't mean just your profit margins. To those who poison our waters indirectly by trashing our streets, using lots of pesticides on their lawns and shampooing five times a day: just stop. To everyone else, pick up other people's trash and stop going through life with your heads in the sand.

I also like to stick my head in the sand. But my favorite thing to do at the beach, next to playing in the clean surf and sand, is to share with my friends a time-honored tradition when the sun goes down: THE BONFIRE. We roast marshmallows, drink wine and see who can light their shoes on fire the longest. Kids, don't do this at home – we are professional idiots. When I see glass and garbage in the sand, I get mad. More importantly, so do the authorities who have the ability to prevent me from enjoying responsible fire on the beach. This happened recently at a beach near me where the Trust that regulates the beach estimated it was costing taxpayers over $100,000 a year just to clean up after people who left their bonfire trash. If you had a fire in your home fireplace, you certainly wouldn't break bottles and leave trash strewn around your living room! There is a saying among campers: LEAVE NO TRACE. That way we can keep the bonfires burning longer. Light Ranger John Muir got this point. So did that Big Papa Bear, American President Teddy Roosevelt.

Commute Your Commute

Lesson: Avoid the jellies and jams! Carpool or take public transport whenever possible. You could catch up on some reading or bring a portable blender and make some new friends very happy, unless there are rules prohibiting blended happiness. There are several online communities for finding carpool riders in your area – keyword 'carpool rides' and '<your town>' into your favorite Internet search engine. Or drive to your local Park & Ride, a pick up joint for riders seeking drivers. Or post a sign at the end of your block that reads, "Driver Seeks Carpoolers for Commute to the Big City. Call Mongo at 415-555-1212."

Lesson: For me, the biggest challenge in taking public transportation has always been the uncertainty. Which bus or train should I take? Where to exit? How long will I have to wait for the next bus or train? Well, I'm here to tell you that there are resources available to you on the Internet that can help you plan your next trip via public transportation. For residents of the Bay Area, California, click on www.transitinfo.org for the answers. I have used the Take Transit Trip Planner twice now and could not be happier with the results. For everybody else, keyword 'public transportation' and '<your city>' in your favorite Internet search engine. Good luck and happy trails!

Public Transportation

Rant: Why would you ride the bus if you didn't believe it could get you to your appointment on time? Friends are always surprised when I say I take the bus. Their impressions are that the bus is always late and smelly-dirty-crazy.

This is not true for every bus but you only need one bus to be smelly-late and those bus riders will tell other potential bus riders who then continue to spread the misconception that the public transportation system is somehow too flawed to ride. And I too have seen smelly-dirty-crazy! At my Van Ness bus stop, a woman told me 'they' had abducted her and screamed that they were still in her brain. I told her 'they' also like to ride the bus and she quickly ducked into the nearest liquor store – one less spooky, kooky *straphanger* to contend with on my Thursday morning commute!

Lesson: I plan ahead now by invoking the ghost of Vince Lombardi and planning to be everywhere half an hour early. If I miss the bus or it misses me, at least I can catch the next bus or grab a cab and still be on time.

Rant: But not everyone can afford to take taxis and they are the ones most at risk if they are late for work and get fired. People rely on the buses! They must be on time!

I got some free James Taylor tickets on Craigslist.com the other night. I grabbed a quick bite near my bus stop, keeping an eye on the street. The bus actually came five minutes early, zooming by my Lombard Street stoop without stopping. It was one of those slow motion moments – me eating my burrito, a salsa dollop rolling down my chinny-chin-chin, as the bus driver laughed loudly, and then was gone. So I waited for 15 minutes past my scheduled time – no bus. Since I had a transfer to make and 15 minutes until the opening act, I opted for a cab. But this was early on a Saturday night in the city and the cabs were not swarming like they would be at closing time. I wandered up to Fillmore and Greenwich where I spotted a nice-looking couple, kitty corner to mine, looking furiously for something up the street...competition!

But they didn't have to be competition. I approached the couple, arms open, "you going downtown?" They were going where I was going so we agreed to go together and doubled our chances for finding a cab, while cutting our expenses in half. Bea-U-tiful!

As a dispatcher for a trucking company, it was my job to make sure that my drivers arrived early or on time to the farm so that the farmer's tomato harvest did not wait too long in the field, increasing the chances of mold developing and the crop being rejected at the inspection station. But when I was short trailers, guys like seven-foot-tall, 250 pound farmer Kidwell would bear down on my fragile little 10 x 10 foot trailer office in his monster truck demanding trailers and respect. And by not delivering on my promise to get trailers to his farm on time, whether it was my fault or not, I was disrespecting him, his family and his farm.

Lesson: The San Francisco Muni system should be run on the same principal. If your bus is late or a no show, let your mayor and supervisors know immediately and loudly. That's their job. They work for you. And if they pay your concerns lip service only, pay 'em back with a visit from farmer Kidwell. Demand respect.

Lesson: Test-drive alternative fuels for the rest of us and let us know about your journey and actual fuel savings and greenhouse gas emissions. What do I mean? Ask Rachel Garlin at www.rachelgarlin.com. She is a teacher who toured the country in a Veggie-Van fueled by french-fry grease. She walks the talk...and then she sings about it.

CHAPTER 10: NOISE POLLUTION

Honk!

Lesson: Lay off the horn!

Rant: City drivers are the worst. Their patience is paper thin while their horns seem razor sharp echoing through the canyons of the concrete jungle. They honk at four-way stops when someone steps out of line. They honk at double-parked cars and jaywalkers. They honk at poor little touristas who can't be helped. They honk just to hear themselves honk! Why do they honk so much? I thought honking was reserved for emergency situations only, like when someone is merging into a blind spot, animals are on the road or the San Francisco Giants have won the pennant. In a small 7 x 7 mile city like San Francisco, all 750,000 of us hear you when you honk.

I would love to see a law that fines audio scofflaws who interrupt my peace. I envision anti-noise pollution signs or some other symbol to warn people that if they lay on the horn, a police officer is going to ticket them. I envision more inventive, less obtrusive car alarms. I envision happy souls walking back from bars quietly and arguing couples finding other places to vent their frustration than outside my bay windows. I'm sleeping here for crying out loud! And while we're on the subject of crying, crying babies should be fined as well. *They can't pay and they don't know the laws?* Ignorance is no excuse for breaking the law! Mothers, how about teaching your babies alternatives to crying to express what they want? I've seen sign language work with my niece quite effectively.

Of course, babies cry for reasons that can't be helped. I'm not a monster!

Leaf blowers

Rant: What's the point in blowing a bunch of leaves away from where they fell? Let them be. They look pretty and make great mulch for gardens. If you have to be a perfectionist, why not use rakes or brooms? Leaf blowers are gas-powered and sound-feel like a chain saw cutting through my brain. I know I'm in the minority here but as more and more people work from their homes and apartments where the wild leaf blowers roam, I gotta imagine we will soon have the numbers to stop this menace to societal sanity.

Lesson: Use a broom. It's cheaper, better exercise and doesn't add to the greenhouse gasses.

Cell phones

Lesson: "Gosh, you have such a beautiful ring tone! Can I see your phone? I just want to see what it sounds like in my water glass." Please, please, please turn off or vibrate your cell phone in a restaurant, during a movie, or anywhere other people go to enjoy something in peace! We go to these places to escape the cold, cruel world, not to invite it in to sit next to us!

CHAPTER 11: ROAD TRIPPING GAMES

Those that don't know the games of life are destined to lose them.

– Unknown

Are we there yet?

If you haven't noticed yet, your children have lots of energy that needs release when traveling. Why is a conservationist recommending road trips in a car? Because it is good for the soul. You need to get away from your familiar surroundings with their famished, familial obligations. If you feel guilt, then make up for it by sacrificing your comfort commute for carpooling or taking public transportation for a week. But for the love of god, get out of the house. Don't forget to stop at your favorite filling station to check the tire pressure. Under-inflated tires can cost you up to 3% of your fuel economy. At today's gas prices, that can mean a savings of $2.50 on a 500 mile trip or $12 per month if you drive 60 miles to work each way. Don't forget to also check your fluid levels – oil, windshield wipers and turn signals.[19]

Road trips provide the ultimate test of parental authority. If you relaxed your authority at home, it's gonna show on the road. But this is also a great opportunity to re-assert that authority with patience, while maintaining everyone's sense of humor. How do you do that? You're the driver, you control the pace and conversation of the trip. Bask in your power! But use it wisely.

Road trips are a great way to educate your children about the world around them. This is important since much of the way we have treated the earth has had to do with ignorance of our effects on it. So get out there and see both the constructive and destructive impacts we have on our world. Bring a box of golf pencils and notepads for everyone to write down what they see.[20] Since they are not SHOUTING out what they see, they will need to provide detail so they can remember it later during show & tell over fried chicken and milkshakes. This game is always on and will never get boring if you provide other games to fill in the cracks between your kids' observations.

Bring lots of car entertainment: coloring books, cards, magic tricks, etc. But keep them hidden in a closed bag! These are your back-up plans should the following games get boring. Whip them out one at a time so your kids don't get overwhelmed and get bored again. Books on CD are always a good call.

Pack a six-pack of bottled water and refill them when needed with tap water at the restaurants and gas stations when you stop. Remember to stay hydrated but don't forget, the more you drink, the more you pee. Unless you have some sort of portable potty on board, you're gonna be stopping a lot. Pack healthy, easy-to-eat snacks, napkins and some plastic supermarket bags to use as trash bags. Bag-Packs?

Stop and explore. If someone spots a big ball 'o twine to climb, go check it out and take pictures of your kids trying to lift it. Bring along some toys like a Frisbee or soccer ball and let your kids burn off some energy. Rest stops usually have expansive, inexpensive grassy play areas perfect for these types of games. You already paid for the sod, you might as well use it, you big sod.

As a last resort to keeping the peace, use bribery. Pack along some coins and offer them to your children in exchange for blessed silence. Now they are rich, independently wealthy precious metal magnets and you are the noise police. Each time they interrupt mom and dad during the adult swim period – the time mom and dad have to share each other's company – the kids lose a coin.

License Plate Game: Who can notice the most U.S. states in a half-hour? One kid keeps score. Since it is on their honor, that they actually saw the plate, it reinforces their sense of trustworthiness – that they can be trusted. Trust in you can be taken to a higher level when you give your children opportunities for you to trust them. Award bonus points for hybrids and other greenish vehicles. Give more bonus points for expired plates. Give super bonus points for glimpsing the driver of a hybrid car with expired plates getting frisked by police on the roadside.

Repeat Letter: First player starts with A: My name is Abby, I live in Arizona, and I like Apples. Next player: My name is Bart, I live in Boise, and I like Beavers. Keep going.

Name that Tree, Flower or Crop: Best for children grades 5 and up who have begun to study the earth sciences. Now it's their turn to teach you something.

Color My Mind: One person thinks of a color intensely, closing his/her eyes until the color is imprinted in her brain, then opens her eyes, stares directly into her partner's eyes, and says "What color am I thinking?" If the two are incredibly in synch, you'd be surprised how often the other person guesses the right color on the first or second guess. Start by using primary colors from the normal spectrum only, graduate up to more diverse palettes. Only up to three color guesses are allowed, then change turns.

Scrapbooks: At every pit stop, be sure to take a moment to pick up a flower, stick, rock, menu, postcard, bottle cap, matchbook, souvenir napkin or orphaned hubcap to press into your road trip scrapbook.

Imagination Time: One person starts off the story, in the most colorful and imaginative way possible, setting the time and location, talking about characters, and in the middle of the sentence she lets the other player take over, continuing the thread of the story but adding his own colorful anecdotes. Then, in the middle of one of his sentences, he passes the story back to her. If you want to play along, record these made-up stories in a notebook because, as hard as you try to remember them forever, they disappear from memory and history as quickly as they are improvised.

Glove Compartment Schwag: Reorganize your glove compartment by emptying its contents and having your kids separate the treasure schwag from the trash.

Capture the Schwag: When road tripping, you need to stop for pits and for sighting the sees. Challenge your kids to capture stuff that does not belong to another person and that has an interesting quality: free postcards at the java chop, a fallen button, a lost dog. Bring plenty of waterless hand cleaner. When you make your nightly stop at the local choke & puke, throw it all in a pile and share your stories. First prize goes to the winner. Second prize goes to the most inventive reuse of the winner's first prize. Third prize goes to the kid that can make his brothers and sisters laugh soda out their noses. And so on.

Truck Stop Schwag: Kids, convince your parents that truck stop food is the best. It usually is pretty good. While you are there, scour the truck store for good schwag. I dig the dome toppers, the billed headrests that say things like, "Bio-Diesel King." The air fresheners are the sweetest I've seen and smelled on the planet. Don't short the candy shop. There's nothing like a sugar-charged road trip to keep the 'rents questioning their 'renting skills'. Go talk to a trucker in the café cuppin' his coffee and munchin' on a chicken pot pie. Some great stories, wise wisdom, those truckers have.

STAGE 6
Talking and Walking Conservation

CHAPTER 12: GET YOUR FEET IN THE DIRT

> "Bum bum bumblebee,
> your honey trips
> keep you at sea."
>
> –*Mongo*

I like to go on walkabout and see all the animals that are still around. It's good exercise, a great way to spend time with friends and allows me to shed the smell of concrete. "Get your feet in the dirt," my friend Adrienne once said. Sometimes I go alone cuz I can feel uncomfortable doing things alone but once I do them, it totally rocks. Author Julia Cameron calls this the "Artist's Date" and recommends artists do this once a week so they experience a time and a place through the first-hand lens of their own eyes, without the subjective views of others. And even if you don't consider yourself to be an artist, trust me, you have one in you. If you decide to hike alone in a desolate area, make sure you bring a walking stick or other means of defense against wild predators, a whistle, water, and warm clothes just in case.

While in the wilderness, I like to take something from nature home with me. Sometimes it's a small rock, sometimes a flower. If flowers perk your petals, then grab a stem from your walkabout and lay it between these pages.

Then close the book to press the plant in place. Keep this 'pressing' as a reminder of the peace and pleasure you received from your hike. Anytime you want to go outside and play but cannot because you have to work or learn in school, take a minute to reopen this page and remember the smells and sounds of that hike. Close your eyes. Take deep breaths. And please only pick one flower – save the rest for the rest of us.

Press the flower you found into these words...onto these words...smudge these words! Test it out by applying half pressure to see how it will layout. At this point, you can still change how it will appear. Once you have the right look, press down firmly. Sit on this book or run it over with your tricycle. If you must press more than one flower, then use any other page in the book you like. Books were meant to be read and used, not to sit in your library like some third place golf trophy.

Insert Nature Here ☐

If you are reading an electronic book, then find another computer monitor and press the flower firmly between the two monitors. Then grab a rubber band... maybe a large rubber band, you know, the kind postal workers carry with them. Better still, take a roll of duct tape and sticky-join the two monitors into a techno-nature sandwich. Definitely hold the mayo. Then, pull the e-book out of your back pocket or purse whenever you need to relax and forget the weight of the world.

Perhaps you are hearing the audio version of this book as you skip down a mountain trail. Take the flower you want to press and stick it up your nose for safe keeping, until you can find another person's nose to stick it in. Ears work too. Now, stop listening to me, remove you ear phones and enjoy the uninterrupted sounds and smells of your hike.

CHAPTER 13: THE CRAFT OF THE CASUAL CONSERVATIONIST

Today, in the United States of America, I believe a lot of people are numbed by all the scary news out there. News of great suffering, war, disease, greed and climate change have many of us running for the shelter of temporary refuges. We don't want to think...to think out the consequences of current events on the world stage or in our own behavior patterns because it just leads to dyspepsia, a bad attitude and doesn't pay the rent or mortgage. We run around with our heads in the sand, which makes it pretty difficult to run at all.

Other people are more enraged by the news, resentful and rebellious against the authorities, the Man or whatever you want to call those people making the rules we all have to follow. We are mad as hell that we don't have ultimate authority over our own lives, our own country and the world. We whine and cry and rail against everything and everyone we perceive to be contributing to the sins of the world. We want you to see our way of thinking right here, right now, or we are going to make a sourpuss face and lay a fat guilt-trip on you.

Then there is the middle of the road where most of us spend our time. We are made up of both kinds of people I just described. We make money, raise families and worry for the future. We shun the destroyers, the liars and the tyranny of evil men. We stand up for what is good and right. We live and let live. We worry for the future, but not at the expense of the present.

But it is hard. The world is not an easy place to live. It wasn't too long ago we were all living hand-to-mouth, meal-to-meal, a constant daily struggle to survive in our caves. In fact, many people still live this way, except the caves are now houses or apartments or the street and the food has already been hunted or grown for you. Even those people who seem to have made it, to be rolling in the big bucks, worry they could return to living a paycheck-to-paycheck lifestyle – it's only one bad business decision, one divorce or one physical injury away.

So how does a human being, not a god – you know, someone that has to live within the rules of gravity, capitalism and reality television – how does someone like this pay the bills AND make a difference in the world?

The Craft of The Casual Conservationist: a way to say more with less.

Instead of thumping people over the head with your own vision of how the world should work, give people the tools and inspiration needed to create their own visions. Talk is cheap so the fewer words you use, the more impact each word will have. Make it known that conservation can be easy and sexy by doing it in front of other people.

Lesson: When I order a beer at a pub, I often ask the bartender if she has any interesting beer caps she can give me. Capture the schwag! If she asks what for, I tell her I'm making a bath loofah, or a mini drum set or some such blather. When I find a cool-looking cap, I whip out my ready-made pin backing, attach it to the cap and give it back to the bartender. Then I make another one and give it to one of the more eager bar patrons watching this exchange. Now people have witnessed a conservation event – not one that will bend steel, but one that just might bend minds. I never explain why – it adds to the mystery.

When building a beer bottle pin, consider the wearer's comfort. If the stem is too long, it will jab them through their clothing. If it's too short, they won't be able to secure the backing. The over-the-counter art store pin sets are often cheaply made so you need to test out each backing to make sure they can be opened and closed easily. The pressure is the key – not enough and you catch on the barb, too much and it will slip right thru your fingers. You will also need some double-sided puffy tape to complete the pin backing. Don't peel off the puffy tape side that will attach to the bottle cap until the last minute.

Wear your bottle cap pin with pride – this is a badge of *The Casual Conservationist.*

Lesson: After a good bottle of wine or liquor, I rinse out my bottle and take it to the local florist for reuse. For less than $5, I now have a unique flower vase that I can give to my mom, my girl or just about anyone on the street who looks sad and lonely. Sometimes I tie a reused bow around the neck of the vase. Just recently, I was able to make three vases under $10 using bottles of vanilla vodka and blackberry schnapps. I gave one to the local coffee shop girl who looked like she could use a smile. It sat lovely on the counter of the coffee shop all week attracting conservation conversations. The other two vases are sitting in my kitchen – two loaded joy torpedoes waiting to be launched.

Lesson: Fast food restaurants are often skimpy on the napkins. They hide them behind the counter and when they do give you one, it is usually small. Hooray for the trees! However, other restaurants give you a bath towel-sized napkin to wipe your dribbles. Whenever I get one of these large, heavy-grade napkins, I perform a little mitosisian parlor trick. I fold the napkin length-wise several times so that it looks like a long pencil and then tear it in half at the middle point. Folding ensures a clean tear. My original napkin now has two nappy kins, one of which I put in my pocket while the other cleans my messy bits and pieces. People always look strangely sideways at me when I perform this trick in public. I like it that way. If only they knew...

Lesson: I had a cold and cough recently and found myself suckling those beautifully-wrapped Ricolah cough drops. The wrapper is fairly flexible, doesn't tear easily and looks nice. So I folded and twisted the wrapper, leaving one end in bloom. Tearing short strips on the bloomy end, I was able to create a mini flower bouquet suitable as a broche, hair-tie for girls with curls or a graveside gift for lost loved ones. I tried giving it to the older lady sitting next to me on the bus but she refused. Doh! I guess one man's art is another woman's trash. These throat soothing bouquets also make a great pick up line, as long as you don't hack up a lung during the delivery.

Lesson: When you have an occasional smoke and there is no ashtray available, simply snuff the ember with a shoed foot, pick the butt back up and deposit it in a trash can or planter box. Make sure that it is fully out, and then make sure that you put it in a place where, should it catch fire, it won't burn anything around it. While you're on the ground, pick up any stray butts you may find. Hopefully there are other smokers watching you do this. Don't forget: the fishies hate butt heads.

Have you created ways to say more with less? Share them with other conservation-minded folks at www.HowToConserve.com.

CHAPTER 14: THE CASUAL CONSERVATION CORPS

> "Everyone wants to be strong and self-sufficient, but nobody is willing to put in the work necessary to achieve these goals"
>
> *– Bapu, a leader better known by another name*

When I saw these words for the first time, I questioned my own commitment to living a better life. Was I walking the talk or just talking the walk? I began to look very closely at my consumption decisions and found that I wasn't the conservationist I thought I was. Sure, I didn't drive my car if I could walk to the store. And I recycled...most of the time. But I realized that if I was any indication of how the rest of the world conserved, we were all in for the longest, hottest summer in history.

So I took my conservation efforts to the next level. I began to bring my used plastic bags with me to the store and I took public transportation more often, even if it meant a little inconvenience. Still, one man alone cannot make a difference unless other people stand with him. So I began to recruit people to the conservation lifestyle.

At first I beat them over the head with doom and gloom. As you probably expected, I was the life of the party. People began to avoid me like the plague. So I changed my tack. I adjusted the way I approached my friends and family to discuss the problems we mutually face. I started to talk solutions. But these were solutions that I heard about or saw on television – not solutions I had actually tried. And every once in a while, someone smarter than me would stop me cold and tell me I was wrong.

I don't like to be wrong. I think it has something to do with my Missouri roots. 'Show me' they say in Springfield and Columbia. I think they even say it on the state license plate. So with 'Show Me' as my new conservation mantra, I changed from teacher to student. And the more I learned from first hand experience or through the eyes of people I trust, the more my conservation message gained meaning. You see, your words reflect the quality of your thoughts and human beings tune into this at a subconscious level.

But while quality thoughts lead to quality words, quality actions speak bigger volumes about who you really are. And I found that my words were much less effective in changing people's minds about conservation than were my actions. When people actually saw me picking up trash and slipping stray rubber bands onto my wrist, they would sometimes do so too. When other people saw me doing weird things with bottle caps, they stopped to ask me why. This opened up the conversation and allowed conservation an opportunity to get a few words in edgewise.

Well, this all took a few years to evolve – I'm a slow learner. But because of all this trial and error, I was able to glimpse some truisms or proverbs or whatever you want to call them, that helped remind me what to do when I forgot what to do. You see, I'm also quite forgetful. But lucky for you, I compensate for my poor memory by writing down just about everything that comes into my head.

As my conservation lifestyle has evolved (and is still evolving), I wrote down a few thoughts here and there which eventually evolved into a code. I don't usually share my personal codes, they are lost on most people, but since you have read this far, you might be considering a greater commitment to conservation and I wish to encourage that sort of thinking in the world. But before I give you this code, I need to know that you are worthy to receive it. That is, I need to know that you have the heart strength, the discipline and the stamina to live by this code.

I need to know that, when those conservation opportunities we talked about earlier arise, you will stand and defend my children's and grandchildren's future, as I pledge to do the same for yours.

If you cannot make this commitment, there's really no reason to read the next chapter. It is a code of teachings that go well beyond the Steps of Stuff. These teachings help me to remember how to conserve and how to teach conservation in an effective way. But please know that there are no hard feelings on my part. I know your life is busy and that survival in this world, even without the threat of global warming and climate change, is no sure bet. I wish you well on *your* way. I know you'll find the rest of the book entertaining and informative.

However, if you accept this commitment, you will find the code in the next chapter to be a valuable asset in your efforts to change more than just your own life. All I ask is that you acknowledge this commitment to yourself by signing the line below and keeping this book in a visible location in your home, as a reminder of your daily commitment to conservation. And it is my great honor to pledge my name beside your name.

____________________ ____________________

(I commit to conservation.) (I commit to conservation.)

CHAPTER 15: THE CODE OF THE CASUAL CONSERVATION CORPS

1. Practice what you know. There's always someone out there smarter than you and if you continue to talk about things you've never tried or someone you trust has never tried, that person is going to find you eventually and make you look like a donkey.
2. Practice what you preach. If you say you are going to do something, do it. If you aren't going to do something, don't say it.
3. Practice your listening skills. We become powerful by the questions we ask, not the answers we give. This was Albert Einstein's Way. This is what geniuses do – they ask lots of questions. I heard someone say once, "If it's not my genius, it's not my job." Make 'listening' your job.
4. Practice loudly. Be a leader and a beacon to anyone who cares to open their hearts to conservation.
5. Practice patience. Your friends and neighbors need to see the benefits of conservation, not thumped over the head with it. The world is going to become a harder place to live and survive. People will be grouchier. They will honk their horns at the slightest grievance. It's back to the Stone Age – a place where patience will be at a premium. Be the light. To find

your patience, meditate or help out an older, slower neighbor or just ask lots of questions. Hear as well as you listen. Don't honk your car horn unnecessarily. Breathe.

6. Practice joy. Conservation is not for the sour-faced man. You will need to keep your spirits high and never forget what it is you are fighting for. Dance. Play an instrument. Slap your knee. Smile at the sun. Smell the anemones. Use what Mother Nature gave you before Father Time takes it away.
7. Practice Kindness. Play nice with all the other kids for you never know when you will need a helping hand. They may have the last lifeboat on the Titanic. This is all about karma. I would not have been able to finish this book and travel America without the help of at least 50 people who gave me their help without thought of receipt.
8. Practice Creativity. *The Casual Conservationist's* Way is but one way to live your life. Invent your own Way to live in harmony with nature.
9. Practice makes perfect. It is through practice that one achieves the skill of a conservation samurai. I, however, am still working on my green belt.
10. Practice thoughtfulness. Never buy something unless you know what its disposal looks like. Is it landfill, oceans or air? How could it be reused? Maybe you don't need it?
11. Practice thankfulness. Enjoy what you got...when you got it. Honor the great people in your life. Things

and people do not last but your memories of them do. No need to keep up with the Joneses. Is their grass really that much greener? It's because they probably use too much pesticide.

12. Stay hydrated – drink lots of water. Stay oxygenated – breathe lots of air. By taking care of your body and your mind, you will be ready to take advantage of the opportunities that await you in a life of conservation.
13. Go out into nature and shout at the top of your lungs RIA (Rye-Ahh)! Shout at the top of your lungs RETAW (Re-tahhh)! These are reminders of how good it is to be alive. This is also a good alternative to honking your auto's horn when you are frustrated.
14. Lead a balanced lifestyle – balance your need to feed with your new need to lead. If you are more concerned with where your next meal is coming from, it will be difficult to focus on conservation. Don't be afraid to ask for help, as long as you are working as hard as you can to be self-reliant.
15. Am I preaching to the choir? Spend time with people who don't see eye-to-eye with you on conservation. Respectfully remind them of what you are fighting for – clean nature to play in, clean water to make lemonade and clean air to breathe. I like to hang out with and date like-minded conservationists. But I do more good by also spending time with good people who just need better information and solutions.

16. Connect with other conservationists in your local area to brainstorm and give each other words of encouragement.
17. Get your feet in the dirt and off the concrete. Go hike a mountain. Walk around a lake. Visit your friends in the country. Bring your kids so they see the real goods in the world. The day people stop getting out of their apartments and homes for some fresh air is the day the music dies.

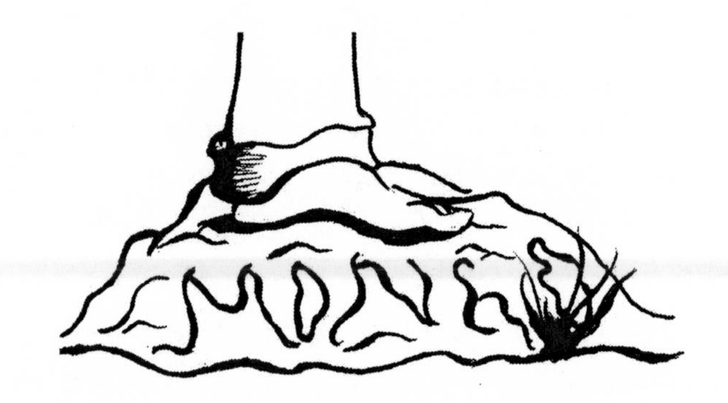

THE END

Yup, you've reached 'The End'. I'm sorry, did you want more? Okay, here are a few more lessons...

Fun With Cats

Lesson: Take an old postal box, the kind you get when you order a book and swiss cheese the thing. Punch out holes all over the box but make sure you can open and close one large hole securely. Fill it up with kitty kibble, throw it near a hungry cat and watch the fur fly.

Lesson: *Corks* make great tent stake protectors, beer bottle plugs and umbrella tip stoppers. I especially dig the umbrella stopper cuz it makes would-be muggers pause and wonder, "Is that umbrella tip loaded?"

When the great outdoors come in doors

Lesson: Yogurt/cottage cheese tubs make great spider cabs. The trick is to capture your arachnid roommate without causing death or lost limbs and to close the lid. Then, when it is convenient, drop off your fare at the nearest tree or bush. Don't wait around for the tip, you ain't getting one. I heard a story recently about an auto shop invasion...by a muskrat. The guys there acted as if the world was ending and subsequently killed the 'rat'. Yoooou dirty rat! Given the increasing loss of animals in the world due to human presence, couldn't they have taken the high road? And I don't mean jumping up on top of their desks screamin' and a shriekin' like they did.

Know your Geography

Lesson: Knowing the geography around your home just may save your life. In the event of flood, where is the high ground? In a tornado, where are the safe places to hide if you are caught on open ground? If a meteorite is coming to take out the planet, what other planet can you escape to? Ok, scratch that last one...for now.

Knowing where nature can be found may save your life, and just might save the earth as well. Can you name the mountain ranges and streams around your house? Can you name the nearest national park area? People want to feel omnipotent, in control, and nature makes us feel out of control. For many of us, our only experience with nature is when it crawls into our bedrooms or thunders down upon our heads. I hear people say all the time, "Man, it sucks outside today," because the sun is not shining. But nature doesn't have to be an inconvenience. Rain is awfully convenient for the farmers who make our food. Rain is terribly convenient for cleaning our streets of grime.

Many people have a mental block about getting out into nature, especially city folks. Many of my fellow San Franciscans won't go anywhere that involves going over a bridge or through a tunnel. Pshaww! Don't stay in your homes, in your easy-set worlds. Get out of the house and into nature! Bring a friend and carpool. By doing so you will better understand what it is we are fighting for and you just might find a sanctuary when mother nature comes looking to whoop your butt!

Get your feet in the dirt (and off the concrete).

Conserve our Traditions

Lesson: As we wander on into the 21st century, we are losing many of our great traditions, like the ability to pick a ripe fruit at the supermarket, how to crochet a sweater or how to make coffee for 1,000 soldiers. Grandpa Ray taught me that trick: take a new steel garbage can, fill it with water over a stove or fire, then add the ground beans, an egg, a tablespoon of salt, boil it and presto! Sounds pretty gross but if it's good enough for World War II vets, it's good enough for me.

Don't lose these stories, they are more valuable than gold and need to be captured and retold to your kids and their kids. So interview your elders, find out what makes 'em crotchety and mean. Find out how Grammy Narcissa found food during the Great Depression. Be respectful, some of these stories are fond memories, while others can be a source of great pain. Respect your elders but get these stories down on paper nonetheless. You honor your elders by passing on their legacy. Then give these books as gifts to your family – the audience that will most enjoy and use this information.

Girlfriend Games

Lesson: Hot Mama Birds – party like its 1955 and take out all those shoes and clothing you rarely wear. Lay them out on the floor and everyone gets to pick one item. Then it's on to round two. Beware! Your girlfriends may want their clothes back when they see you out looking oh so fabuloso. Wear your conservation with style!

> "Alone of human beings, the good and wise mother stands on a plane of equal honor with the bravest soldier; for she has gladly gone down to the brink of the chasm of darkness to bring back the children in whose hands rests the future of the years."
>
> *– Big Papa Bear American President Theodore Roosevelt, The Great Adventure, 1918*

Lesson: Ladies. Stop grossing out your men by leaving hair all over the bathroom. Harvest your hair brush and attach those tangles to your birdfeeder so birds can one-stop shop for their food AND their nest. No bird feeder? Get the kids to build one using those non-recyclable milk cartons...easy.

Lesson: Take your clean, empty egg carton, grab some seeds or small pebbles and do the Mancala! This 'count and capture' game has been dated archaeologically to 6th century Eritrea and Ethiopia. It is a great game for teaching children to count and play nice. Key word 'Mancala' in your favorite search engine for instructions on how to play.

Lesson: Hearsay is heresy. Conserve people's good names by not engaging in gossip about them behind their backs. Never say something negative about someone unless he is present or has an opportunity to defend himself. This is what people mean when they talk about *character.* This is what they mean when they talk about *honor.*

Minimal Effort Night (MEN)

Lesson: Every man should have MENs night – one night a week with absolutely no commitments to be concerned with. You cannot ask him to do dishes, vacuum carpets or take out the trash. Foot-rubs are negotiable. If he wants to go out with his friends, there will be no asking about where he's going or what time he's coming home. This is about relationship conservation by building trust and building longing. Plus it is the nature of men – we need to roam and find adventure! Men, don't breach this trust or you are gonna make me look bad in front of the ladies. Ladies, you should have one of these nights too!

Lesson: Parking cones make great tip jars. Attach a bottom, paint the sides brown, add some lava effects and presto...Mount Tipwell!

Mind Conservation

Lesson: If you find you get easily bored or distracted in the real world or you need refuge from stress and life's downturns, meditation is an excellent alternative to smoking, tearing out your hair or kicking the dog.

Meditation, a type of yoga, is about going inside yourself, not to sleep, but to awaken interest in yourself.

Somebody asked me the other day why I meditated. For me, meditation is like slowing down the car in order to make a turn. I want to keep my wheels on the pavement while I try to negotiate the change in the road, so I slow down. Whenever I need to make a change in my life, I slow down the world so I can make the change safely, without stress to distract me into making a bad decision. How many of your bad decisions can you blame on stress?

For me, meditation is about shutting out the outside world, opening my ears to the inside world and showing interest in my wild horse thoughts. Many of those raw thoughts ended up in this book. After riding those wild horses, I grow a bit tired and find a certain peace in the silence of my wordlessness. It's like that moment after working out when you finally get home, sit down and soak in the aaaaaahhhhchy endorphins. Then, I begin to practice my *yoga* by concentrating on a word like *peace* or *love.* I ask myself silently, "What is peace?" but I do not give an answer. Instead I let my mind go on walk-about and go where it wills. And boy does it go to some strange and interesting places!

Well, that's it so far for me. After THIS, there is supposed to be an epiphany, some kinda 'AHA' moment but I've never been there. The rucksack Buddhist Jean-Louis Lebris de Kerouac once observed, "obtaining nirvana is like locating silence."

By the way, the word Yoga doesn't mean 'painful body contortions' as I thought it did. Yoga literally means 'union'.

For the kind of yoga I practice, I sit down in a comfortable position, usually in a chair or other posture-supporting contrivance. I shut down my conscious mind and allow a 'union' to begin between my unconscious mind and my soul, that priceless fortune the old devil is always trying to steal. And god willing, the devil's gold-fiddle temptations will find few purchases in me.

Conserve Your Teeth

Lesson: Floss once a day, every 24 hours or after each rotation of the sun. As I just discovered, flossing is your best defense against gum disease and ultimately, tooth loss! Ask your dentist about this. Don't forget to toss that floss into the garbage – better it should land in the landfill than in the ocean or on my front porch!

THE END!

It was good talking with ya'll. I'm on my way to the next town to spread the word on casual conservation. If the good Lord's willing and the river don't rise, I'll see you again. What, you want more? Here's a cupola more rrrrrrrrants...

> "There are two things that I want you to make up your minds to: first, that you are going to have a good time as long as you live—I have no use for the sour-faced man—and next, that you are going to do something worthwhile, that you are going to work hard and do the things you set out to do."
>
> *–President Theodore Roosevelt, talk to school children in Oyster Bay, Christmastime 1898*

Self-reliance

Rant: This came from a man who, with a would-be assassin's bullet still lodged in his chest, delivered a 90 minute speech in Milwaukee, Wisconsin in 1910. Imagine that!

The lesson here is that you cannot wait for others to tell you what to do. Use your moral compass and your creativity. Use your own hands and your own words. Use whatever you got, where you are at, to get where you need to go. Be self-reliant!

This reminds me of the bum-bum-bumblebee. The portly bumblebee has a relatively small wing-to-body mass ratio. By all accounts, the bumblebee should not be able to fly. Yet it finds a way.

You may not be rich, you may not be smart and you may not be good looking. But if you work hard and never give up, you too can find a way to fly, you beautiful bee!

Conservation vs. Capitalism

Rant: There is no fundamental feud between conservation and capitalism. But then why do these two philosophies always seem to be feuding? Why can't we have both a strong economy *and* clean, healthy places in which to live, work and play? Are they mutually exclusive? I wish I knew the answer, but let's explore the debate a bit.

I believe it is only the short-sighted folks, on both ends of the argument, who think capitalism always hurts the environment and who think conservation always hurts the economy. This is just not true...all of the time.

It is true that capitalists protect their gains – capitalists made up of small business people, shareholders of corporations, and the great industrial families. They fought tooth and nail to build up their businesses and they fight voraciously to keep them, sometimes at the expense of the environment and sometimes in union with nature. It is only human nature to protect what you got.

Common folk are no different – you keep a job, one you may or may not like, because you don't want to lose what you have gained and your wife and children need to be able to see the doctor. You seek security for yourself and your family. The company you work for may be working at the expense of the environment or may be working in union with nature. But you keep working because you need the job. This too is only human nature.

And what am I talking about when I say, "This is only human nature?" It is our evolutionary instinct to protect our families, our money, our land and our stuff. And America has gotten good at this. We have one of the highest per capita incomes in the world. We have low unemployment and few people hungry for food, relative to the rest of the world. We have a strong military who has not forgotten the lessons of wars fought on our soil against Great Britain and Mexico and in our waters against Revolutionary France and Spain, as we fulfilled our Manifest Destiny. Nor has our military forgotten how our isolationism leading up to World War I and II nearly lost it all. We fought two Barbary Wars in the early 1800s against a bunch of North African States just to ensure the safety of American trade goods through a Mediterranean Sea threatened by piracy. We fought the Koreans and Vietnamese, and by proxy Russia and China, to ensure capitalism won out over communism. We have evolved into a nation that protects its people, its economy and its way of life by taking the fight abroad. This is our American history.

Not only is this our history but it is the history of the world. Countries are just groups of people that have come together to protect the common interest, to protect their gains through a strong economy and to protect their borders through force of arms.

Countries seek to protect their gains and people by taking the fight outside their borders, where loss of civilian life and infrastructure damage happens to the other guy. They do this because they remember a time when some other country brought a fight to their borders. This is the history of the United States, England, China, France, and Russia, as well as countless others all over the globe. As for the U.S., we have fought the English, the French, the Spanish, and the Mexicans *on* our streets. Of course, *those* streets were once *their* streets but that too is the nature of people and countries. Watch China and India over the next 50 years and you may see this principal repeated.

For a time, the United States was reluctant to step out into the world, to bring the fight to our enemies because we didn't even look at them as enemies – 'we' being popular opinion. Then World War I came around, the Germans were advancing on Europe and we realized we could either fight them here or there. World War II was much of the same. Following WWII, we began in earnest to take our fights outside our borders, to stop our isolationist ways.

And the world is no longer defined by countries as much anymore. We are now defined by military alliances like NATO, the United Nations and many other groupings. We are defined by economic clubs like the North American Free-Trade Association (NAFTA) and the European Union (EU). This concept of a *global economy* is intimately wrapped up in these alliances because it is through strength-of-numbers that countries find security and it is through peace that goods and services can flow. World wars impede the economic flow, causing higher prices and shortages, as well as untold human horror.

However, it is fact that war can also help the economies of the victors through war-time spending and the negotiation of the armistice afterwards. And while we generally think of war in terms of the defense of physical borders, the written history of warfare shows that economic reasons are often behind the push for war. And so it is today, wars are fought by alliances of countries made up of people whose nature it is to defend their families and their gains. In a sense, money protects itself.

And now, the great business empires of old have given way to corporations whose legal structure protects the personal assets of its shareholders. Money protects itself. These corporations are managed by a board of directors whose purpose is to protect the interests of shareholders. This means protect their *money*, with quarterly profits in mind. *What have you done for me lately!* But it also means that corporations protect their shareholders' children's inheritance. While *inheritance* means 'money', it could and should also mean 'quality of life'. Unfortunately, this is harder to measure and communicate to shareholders. Someone should start a business making this communication easier!

Some people argue that the current global economic approach to trading goods and services promotes the corporate model of business while handicapping small business people and their families. Plus, that it allows corporations to move outside their countries of origin to do their dirty business in other countries' backyards. I have heard of environmental catastrophe in far away lands at the hands of alien corporations and I don't like to think I may have supported that in some way.

There are many examples of businesses whose money-centered philosophies have led to environmental damage in our own country as well – poisoned streams, poisoned lands. This has been an indirect result of crazy consumer demand for their products while some companies just dumped waste directly into our streams, rivers and oceans. I will not name names here but you know who you are. If you are struggling with the ethics and economics needed to make the change, know that I support your efforts to change...for you *must* change. I know that it is costly to clean up the past and carries a risk of litigation to admit wrong, but please find a way to clean up your mess when you are done playing with your toys.

And let us not be confused here – businesses who go green may find their costs to be higher than their non-conservation-minded competitors. This is a paradox – doing the right thing can mean your business goes out of business. I think this is the reason industry has been so slow to change. Government could step in here and level the playing field by mandating certain conservation practices. But if we wait around for that to happen, it could be too late! So support those businesses making significant efforts to change, even if that means paying a little extra for their products. If it is a lot extra, then do what you got to do to feed your family.

On the other side of the aisle, the extreme fringe of the environmental movement is trying to preserve what's left of nature and her inhabitants. I use the word *preserve* and not *conserve* because they are going for a 'no participation' approach. On the surface, most of us can agree with the problem they are addressing but too often they overreach in their solutions either because they are true preservationists or they are seeking to build a negotiating position for when it comes time to compromise with the capitalists.

But there are times when this 'overreach' borders on foolhardiness. Timber cutting is an excellent example of this. Hardcore environmentalists chain themselves to trees, lie in front of bulldozers, employ legal tactics to delay and derail timber companies' efforts. Why? Because in the not so distant past, timber companies had free reign to cut what they wanted and some went hog wild in a way that didn't support forest re-growth. When regulations were implemented, some used loopholes or outright scoffed the law to cut more trees.

So environmentalists reacted by fighting for preservation...not conservation. The result? Timber companies cannot get into the forests as much as before and therefore, cannot cut down our trees. But another result is that timber companies cannot harvest fallen trees, which adds more fuel for forest fires and pests.

One of the more devastating pests today is the Mountain Pine Beetle, which has ravaged the pine tree from Jasper National Park in Canada to the San Bernadino National Forest in Southern California. This bug has gone farther north than ever before in recorded history, eating the inner-bark of trees, cutting off their nutrients and water and finally killing them. Why? It is believed that warming winter temperatures in North America have eliminated the yearly freeze that used to cull the beetle herds, coupled with a whole lotta fuel – fallen trees that could have been used to make this book!

There's a feeling out there among a whole lotta people that conservation is anti-business, and others who believe that business is anti-conservation. These stereotypes are not entirely unjustified, as discussed above. But we must bring the two camps together, to rise up against a mutual enemy – the loss of our beautiful world, our Way of life. The world is not a perfect place. But it is still beautiful to me. Our Way of Life is not a perfect way. But it is all I have known and I won't sit idly by while I continue to contribute to its disappearance.

It can be costly for a business owner to change. And, as *The Casual Conservationist* points out, it can be costly not to change for all of us in the long run. But it doesn't have to always be this way. Many companies have reduced their footprints in response to their customers' wishes, their childrens' wishes and the wishes of their consciences. Bravo to them! Will it be enough? Time will tell.

And remember, you have to make money to live but you don't have to live just to make money. This is the great challenge of our generation. What would Big Papa Bear do?

So, Uncle Ebenizer...No Presents This Year?

Rant: Absolutely not! We should celebrate our friends and family with an expression of love, appreciation and joy. However, that expression is insincere unless it has been conceived, packaged and delivered in a manner considerate of the recipients' green. I am pointing no fingers in this book...not at business, government, my friends or my family. I'm merely asking that you consider your actions, display forethought or mindfulness, and above all else, vote with your pocketbook. It's not difficult to balance your need to give to others with your responsibility to conserve green. It is in everyone's best interest that you do both. My wise father once taught me to spend my money on appreciating, and not depreciating, assets. Well, there is no greater appreciating asset on the earth, than the earth. There is a limited supply of land and resources available to us. True, we are continually learning to use those resources more efficiently but they are still decreasing nonetheless.

We accumulate so much stuff during our lives that we end up either trashing or storing much of it. This is like paying tax twice on the same item...once on purchase and once on disposal. True, some stuff just gets old and needs to be replaced. But when you buy quality, you end up buying less quantity.

This lesson was lost on me when I bought a set of cheap kitchen knives several years back. Now, the serrated edges are dull and I have no way of sharpening the blades myself. You see, serrated blades cannot be sharpened using a sharpening stone. You must have each individual edge sharpened professionally and at some cost – the clerk at my local hardware store pointed that one out. It's a pain to cut food and a bit of a safety hazard to boot – I could cut off a finger! Next year, I will be purchasing a higher quality set, one that I can personally sharpen the blades. In the end, I will end up buying two knife sets while adding to our tax bill. For a guy who talks a lot a green, I still have a lot to learn. At least I still have all my fingers.

THE END?

Seriously guys, I got places to be. But I can answer one last question...

What is energy and what does it have to do with greenhouses?

WARNING: This answer is chockful of researched facts 'n' figures. If you are a casual narcoleptic who faints at the site of number crunching, please move on – nothing to see.

Crunch! Crunch! Crunch!

The heat value of fuel, or 'energy', is measured in many ways: barrels or gallons for oil, cubic feet for natural gas, tons for coal, and kilowatt-hours for electricity. These measurements do not include the energy it took to create a particular fuel, although some other fuel was consumed to do so. It also does not include the energy used in transporting that fuel to the end user, like diesel gasoline in an 18-wheeler. And it does not include the energy lost by inefficient creation (e.g. old coal-fired electrical plants), inefficient transportation methods (e.g. power line loss) and inefficient appliances (e.g. old light bulbs). These measurements merely tell you the heat value potential of a fuel.

So how can you compare the energy output between different types of fuel? In America, these measurements are typically converted into *BTUs*, or British Thermal Units. A *BTU* is defined as the amount of heat required to raise the temperature of one pound of water by one degree Fahrenheit. If you look at the manufacturer information on the side of a typical window air conditioner, the capacity of that machine is 10,000 BTUs. An air conditioner with a higher BTU rating can cool more of your house or office. If you would like to convert the heat value of oil barrels or some other fuel to BTU, please keyword 'Energy Conversion Calculator' into your favorite search engine.

So why is this important? Because understanding the BTU values of different fuels will enable you to make an apples-to-apples comparison of how much direct energy you use in your home and at work.

In the year 2006, America consumed approximately 100 QB or Quadrillion BTU of energy. A 'quadrillion' is a whole lotta zeros – 15 to be exact. On average, each person in America consumes 910,000 BTUs of energy each day. You heat or cool your home, drive to work and cook your dinner, all using this energy. And where does it all come from? It comes from the following sources:

- 61% from fossil fuels like coal/used tires, natural gas and petroleum
- 9% from electricity (created using all the other fuels)
- 6% from nuclear energy
- 5% from renewable energy sources like biomass (e.g. ethanol), geothermal (e.g. hot springs), hydroelectric (e.g. dams), solar and wind

- Less than 1% from electricity net imports (we buy a little more electricity from other countries than we sell to other countries)

Note: 67% of the energy used to produce electricity is considered an electric system energy loss made up of natural conversion losses (e.g. steam used to turn electric generators), line losses (electricity lost during transport over the electrical lines) and unaccounted for electricity (ghost food?).

Note: Crude oil makes up 23% of the energy we use and 66% of that is imported oil from other countries. Another way to look at it – *oil imports make up 15% of the total energy we use.*

And where does all this energy go?

- 28% into electric power production (energy to produce energy)
- 23% into industrial production (e.g. the factories that build your car)
- 20% into transportation (e.g. driving your car or truck)
- 15% into residential consumption (e.g. heating your house)
- 13% into commercial consumption (e.g. cooling your office)

Note: Since 1980, all energy consumption sectors have seen growth in energy use between 33% (residential) and 70% (commercial), except for industrial production, which has experienced no significant growth in energy use. This is possibly due to our shift away from manufacturing to an information-based economy as well as more efficient production methods.

Note: The electric power production industry and industrial producers lead all economic sectors in their use of renewable energy at 8% of their total energy usage. The remaining sectors (residential, commercial and transportation) use renewable energy in 2% of their total energy use.

How does this all relate to the greenhouse effect? Energy use produces different amounts of the gasses that contribute to the green house effect. Each economic sector produces roughly the same percentage of carbon dioxide as its percentage of energy consumption. You could say that transportation produces 20% of the carbon dioxide emitted into the atmosphere, as well as using 20% of the energy produced.

There are two other major greenhouse gasses. *Methane* is produced largely by our landfills, farm animal fart 'n' poop, and energy source extraction like coal mining and natural gas/petroleum production, processing and distribution. *Nitrous Oxide* is produced largely by agricultural sources (fertilization and farm animal poop) and automobile emissions.

Energy consumers from the above-mentioned economic sectors choose energy most often based on price or price per kilowatt/hour (kWh). Some choose energy based on how little it pollutes, regardless of price. Some seem to have no choice, like gasoline-powered automobile users. And still others just like to watch the windmill go round and round – it's pretty.

Coal is one of the cheaper fuels and has not seen the recently steep price increases that oil and natural gas have seen. In 2006 America, coal was used mostly in electric power production as well as a little in industrial production at $0.006/kWh (less than one cent!). Despite its heavy contribution to greenhouse gasses (double that of gasoline and natural gas), coal continues to be used heavily around the world for energy production because it is so cheap.

Petroleum (gasoline) is used mostly in transportation and industrial production, with a little being used in residential, commercial and electrical power production. The average price in 2006 for unleaded gasoline was $2.60 per gallon, which translates into $0.07 per kWh. What is the kWh for gasoline at $3.60 per gallon?

Natural gas is used mostly in industrial and electrical power production, with significant amounts used in residential and commercial consumption. In 2006, the average price for residential consumption was $0.05 per kWh.

Electricity, which is made from burning coal, car tires, petroleum and natural gas, as well as other sources like nuclear, wind and solar had an average price in 2006 of $0.10 per kWh. Except for the transportation sector (almost none), electricity was consumed in nearly equal amounts among the remaining sectors. Of course, little-to-no electricity is used to make electricity, thank heavens.

So there's the skinny and fat of energy. The economics of energy are no different than the economics of any other good or service – supply and demand rules, as long as no monopolies or oligopolies exist. The less the world uses, the lower the price (all other factors staying constant) and the less greenhouse gasses are emitted.

Green Attitudes Deserve Gratitudes

These people, things and ideas are the light for me – the green light. It is because of them I had the confidence, discipline and endurance to finish *The Casual Conservationist* and deliver it to my soon-to-be-new friends all over America. Maybe...just maybe...they can be the green light for you too.

Adrienne Biggs, without whose help and inspiration I would never have made it this far

The image of the bumper boats in *Life's Golden Ticket*, by Brendon Burchard (a must read!)

Kiwanis International for helping me set my sights on service

My amazing non-life coach and friend, Mollie Cudmore

Mom and Dad, your labor bore this fruit

Truth for its own sake

The Landlord God...the rest of us are just renting time here. Thanks for helping me find my own voice.

John Denver for the music in his heart

The Sacramento Entrepreneurship Academy at www.sealink.org. If you got the patience and the will, these guys will give you the tools to walk your own path.

Big Papa Bear walking softly and carrying a big stick

San Francisco – the city I live to dream

The crew at SF's All Star Donuts on Chestnut Street for their 24-hour nourishment...Barbara, thanks for finally asking me if I even want a bag – you rawk!

Balloonboy for spreading the joy in his heart and lungs

Blanketman for reminding me that other people have other ways to live and that the road will really rise up to meet you...if you only let it.

Streamerman/Walkingman for teaching me that San Francisco is only 7 by 7 miles

Bushman for scaring the bajeebus out of my tourist friends and making their stay a bit more interesting

Redman for looking after the neighborhood all day and for not asking me to buy him coffee anymore

Flynn for teaching me never to cheat my feet

Ansel Adams and his eye for nature

John Muir and his pen for nature

Dr. Janet Schwartz, my high school English teacher who defined what it *really* meant to teach...sorry for all the dangling modifiers and smelly spellies – it couldn't be helped

My soccer coach Rob Crowley for the fire in my belly – you are missed

Jean-Louis Lebris de Kerouac, long live the legend of Dulouz

Laurel Adams, an amazing bum-bum-bumblebee

My wise grandmas and grandpas

Denise Burchard and her crazy cat

Oprah and the *way* she cares

The Boy Scouts of America and my den mother Mrs. Cornelius for all the Kool-Aid and cookies.

Pandora Internet Radio, I-Tunes and 102.1 for the inspirational licks...save Internet Radio!

Save Net Neutrality! None of this would have been possible if the prices had been higher.

Paula & Jim, thanks for the backpack – maybe I can return it during the road trip?

Uncle J and our dinner table chats

Cousin JR for walking the line all these years – you are a rawkin' inspiration.

Mariko Nabori

Cindy Fisher, The Write Life Coach

Vladislove and his present of presence

Annie Parker, a great friend

Pioneer Rachel Garlin and her grease-fueled, inspiration-driven bus

Alexis Summerfield, Clouds of Purple Chi

Kelly Smolen

Alamo's Dr. Ken Soult D.D.S. and Rotary International for helping me achieve my teenage goal of playing soccer in Sweden

Bill "Whoop-out" Mohr and my CCIM education

David Burchard

Mari Barfs!

Demanda

Darsie and Dr. John Swanson

Rudy and Kelly Gelenter

Erica P.

AAA-grade Peter Monie

Gonzo #589

Tone!

Toastmasters International for helping me to talk good

Jana Byrd

Rizzo!

Amy Mosebach

Vook

San Francisco's toothy truthsayer Dr. Alexander Farr, D.D.S. for teaching me some flossing rationale I could really sink my teeth into

David Kordsmeier

Holy Toledo, a real-life creative vortex!

My Baker Street meditations

Ed Becnel for the great encouragement

The Grove's Mount Pinto standing tall with open arms

Libby Patterson

Paula Nichols

JOURNAL

Remember your own conservation inventions or share them with the next reader, write here!

ABOUT THE AUTHOR

Eric Mongo Robbins is a dreamer with his head in the clouds, and his feet firmly rooted in the ground. It's quite a stretch. His roots can be traced back to the Colorado Rocky Mountains and to the muddy Missouri banks of the Mississippi River. Mongo currently lives in Northern California – cornered by towering Mount Diablo, wind-swept Mount Tamalpais and the cold Pacific Blue. There he can be found snowboarding the Sierra Nevada, hiking near his home or playing soccer with his inmates.

Mongo received a formal education in entrepreneurship and economics in the 1990s. He received an informal education in conservation from many sources throughout his life but he credits his grandmother most with tuning his eyes and ears into the subject. Mongo has worked in journalism, public relations, commercial real estate and the transportation sector. Transportation sector? Actually, Mongo drove 18-wheelers up and down California's breadbasket, the Central Valley, hauling tomatoes that probably ended up on your dinner table or, if you got too close, on your windshield!

When Mongo is not working or enjoying the company of friends, he is volunteering his time with Little Brothers/ Friends of the Elderly driving older folks to their medical appointments. He also works with Wherever The Need USA and the Poetry For Water fundraiser, helping raise money for folks in Africa so they can provide themselves with clean drinking water. Mongo also supports Kiwanis International and their efforts to make the world a better place for children. But he wasn't always this way.

SO WHAT qualifies Mongo to get up on his soapbox and tell YOU how to conserve? That's the beauty of this thing...nothing! He's just like you. Mongo holds no special degrees or licenses in the environmental sciences. Mongo is not exactly on a mission from God. He just wants to help people see that they have the ability to make a difference, which can be done without sacrificing too much of their time or money. In fact, you often save time and money by conserving! And Mongo wants to make conservation beautiful. Mongo believes that beauty is a product of how much water you drink, how much care you dare to share and how much joy you allow into your life.

END NOTES

1. I played with this name for some time. Should it be "98% of the scientific community" or "a gaggle of scientists?" The challenge is that there has never been a complete survey of the world-wide scientific community on climate change and global warming. There have been smaller, but still large, surveys done by the Intergovernmental Panel on Climate Change (IPCC) and many scientists have appeared in print, radio, television and the Internet agreeing with the IPCC consensus. Still, there are a few scientists who believe that global warming is not really happening and a few more scientists who believe that global warming is happening but that man is not the cause. But from my viewpoint, these scientists appear to be in the minority of scientists who are actually speaking out on the subject. While coming to a consensus based on an incomplete survey is not the most "scientific" way to reach a conclusion, it is the best data we have today. And given the risks involved, I felt comfortable saying that a majority of scientists believe global warming is happening and that Man is the cause.

2. Conservation. Dictionary.com. Dictionary.com Unabridged (v 1.1). Random House, Inc. http://dictionary.reference.com/browse/conservation (accessed: April 25, 2007).
3. Preservation. Dictionary.com. *The American Heritage® Dictionary of the English Language, Fourth Edition.* Houghton Mifflin Company, 2004. http://dictionary.reference.com/browse/preservation (accessed: April 25, 2007).
4. The U.S. Environmental Protection Agency, Municipal Solid Waste, Basic Facts at http://www.epa.gov/epaoswer/non-hw/muncpl/facts.html
5. The Environmental Protection Agency (EPA)
6. http://www.epa.gov/epaoswer/non-hw/muncpl/ghg/climpayt.pdf
7. www.epa.gov/epaoswer/non-hw/reduce/catbook/compost.htm
8. The U.S. Geological Survey Water Science for Schools at http://ga.water.usgs.gov/edu/graphic-shtml/summary95.html
9. World Water Resources And Their Use, Joint Shi/Unesco Product, Information about world water use & water availability, calculated group of sciences in State Hydrological Institute (St.-Petersburg, Russia) by edition of I.Shiklomanov, Table 17 (3) at http://espejo.unesco.org.uy/part'3/html/tb_17'3.html.
10. Omitted
11. www.watercasa.org

12. www.watercasa.org
13. United States Postal Service 2006 Annual Report, Financial Highlights at http://www.usps.com/financials/_pdf/anrpt2006_final.pdf
14. The Center for Development of Recycling at http://recyclestuff.org/JunkMail.asp and The Office of Compliance Assistance and Pollution Prevention, Ohio Environmental Protection Agency at http://www.epa.state.oh.us/opp/consumer/junkmail.html
15. www.obviously.com/junkmail/
16. The Center for Development of Recycling at http://recyclestuff.org/JunkMail.asp.
17. http://www.eia.doe.gov/emeu/mer/consump.html
18. U.S. Department of Energy, Energy Efficiency and Renewable Energy, Information Resources, U.S. Energy Statistics, http://www.eere.energy.gov/states/us_energy_statistics.cfm. Avg. kWh/person/yr (2001 adjusted to 2003 at 1.4%/yr): 4,342 times avg. cost/kWh (2003): $0.087 equals $378/person/yr.
19. Turn signal fluid levels are an oft misunderstood mechanism of motor vehicles. Most mechanics don't even understand this part of the car and will try to hide their ignorance by telling you it doesn't exist. However, you can usually find the turn signal fluid reservoir behind the automatic ash tray extinguisher or the arm rest air bag. Yes, I'm kidding.
20. Pencil marks on the leather can be erased easier than pen marks.

21. All this information can be mined at:
    http://www.eia.doe.gov/emeu/aer/envir.html
    http://www.eia.doe.gov/emeu/mer/prices.html
    http://www.eia.doe.gov/emeu/mer/consump.html
    http://www.eia.doe.gov/kids/energyfacts/science/energy_calculator.html

    My numbers may not coincide exactly with the information produced by the U.S. Energy Information Administration (EIA), but they are pretty close...close enough to give you an accurate representation of where energy comes from and where it goes. The reports listed above are based on supply surveys – that is, the information contained within these reports was provided by the suppliers and marketers of energy. If you mine these surveys yourself, you will find that the same data category can contain different results at different points in the reports. However, the differences are generally marginal. Also, these results will most likely differ from the results of consumption surveys or reports provided by the end users of energy. As you can probably tell, end-user surveys are more difficult to obtain given that there are a lot more consumers than there are producers.

22. 100QB divided by 300 Million Americans divided by 365 days in the year

Printed in the United States
84654LV00001B/163-237/A

9 780979 727405